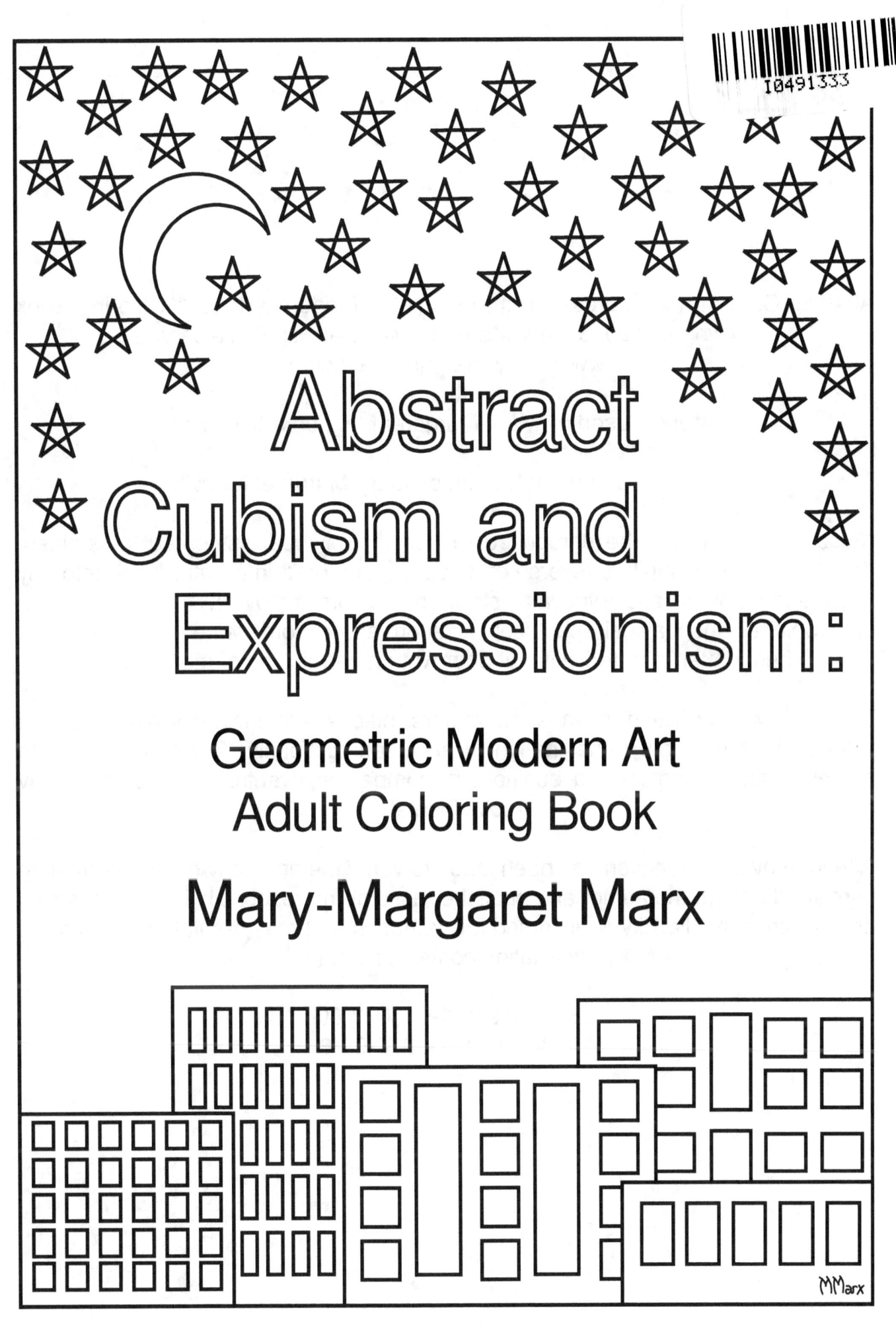

Abstract Cubism and Expressionism:

Geometric Modern Art
Adult Coloring Book

Mary-Margaret Marx

ISBN-13: 978-1-945078-00-2
ISBN-10: 1-945078-00-6

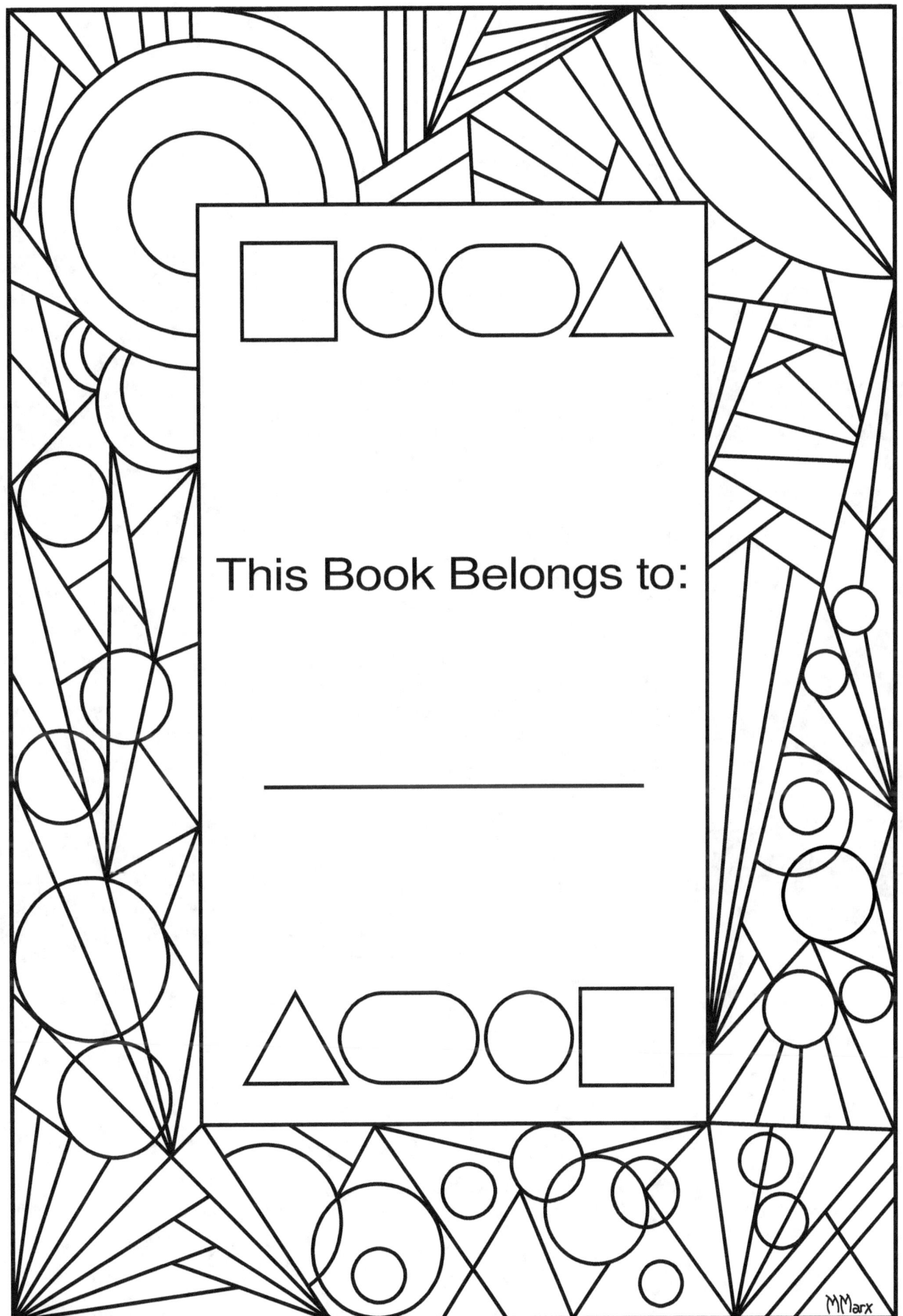

This Book Belongs to:

_____

Introduction

I have always been fascinated with Abstract Art, Cubism, and Expressionism. Artists experimented with geometric shapes, color, and placement to evoke emotion. As you look at this art from different angles, the shapes and colors merge into different arrangements. No one sees the same thing.

In your hands, you hold my version of these art styles. I have always been drawn to geometric shapes. I love to use them in repeating patterns. With placement and color, geometric shapes take on different forms.

There are 40 of my original designs in this book. There are two bonus pages of bookmarks. At the back of this book are two pages that you can use to test your colors. All designs are single-sided, but I recommend putting extra paper behind the design you are working on so that the colors and indentations do not pass through onto the next design.

Words cannot express my thanks for your purchase of this book. I am both happy and humbled that you have chosen this book. I wish you many hours of happiness and creativity.

MMarx

Mary-Margaret Marx
www.mary-margaretmarx.com

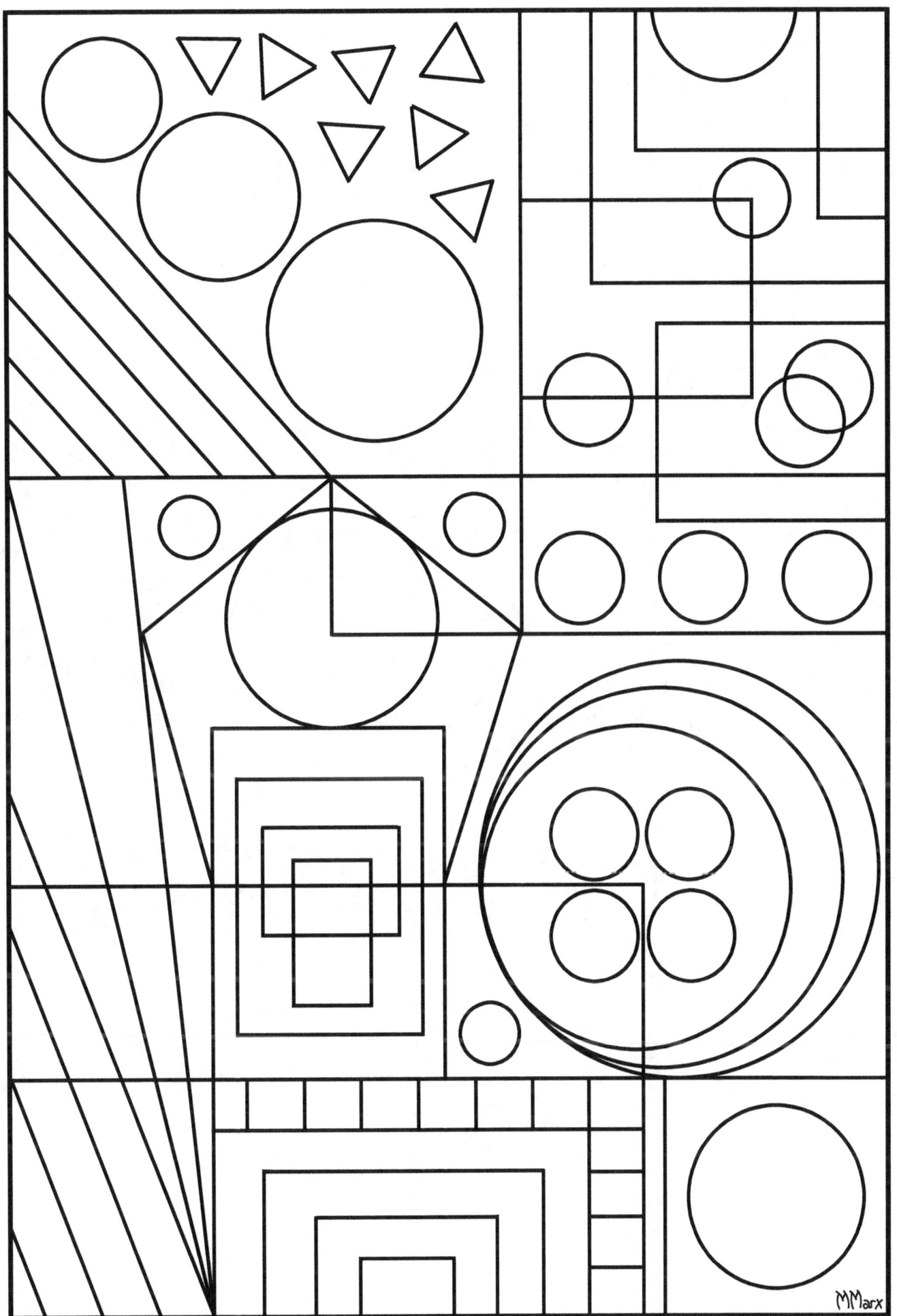

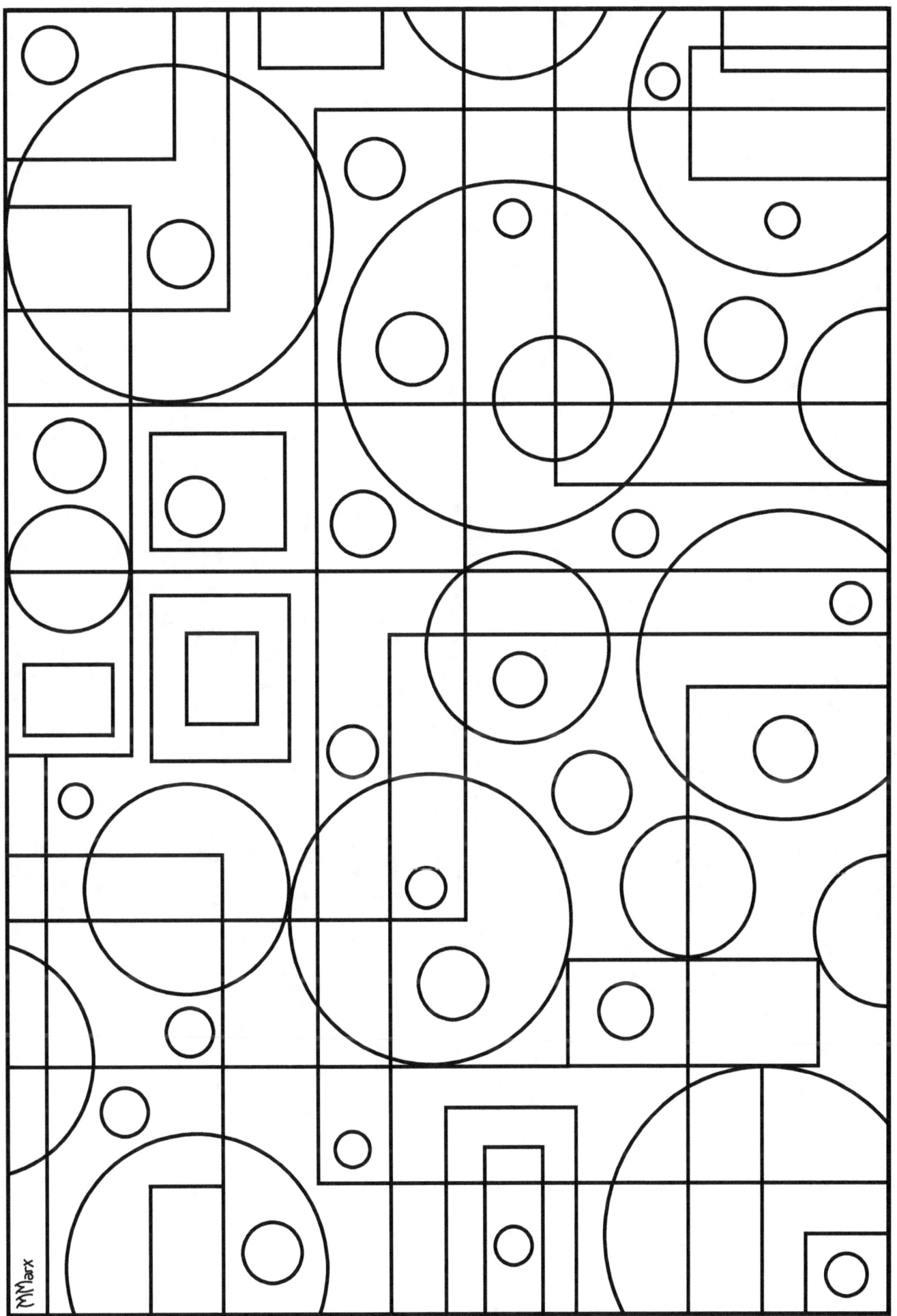

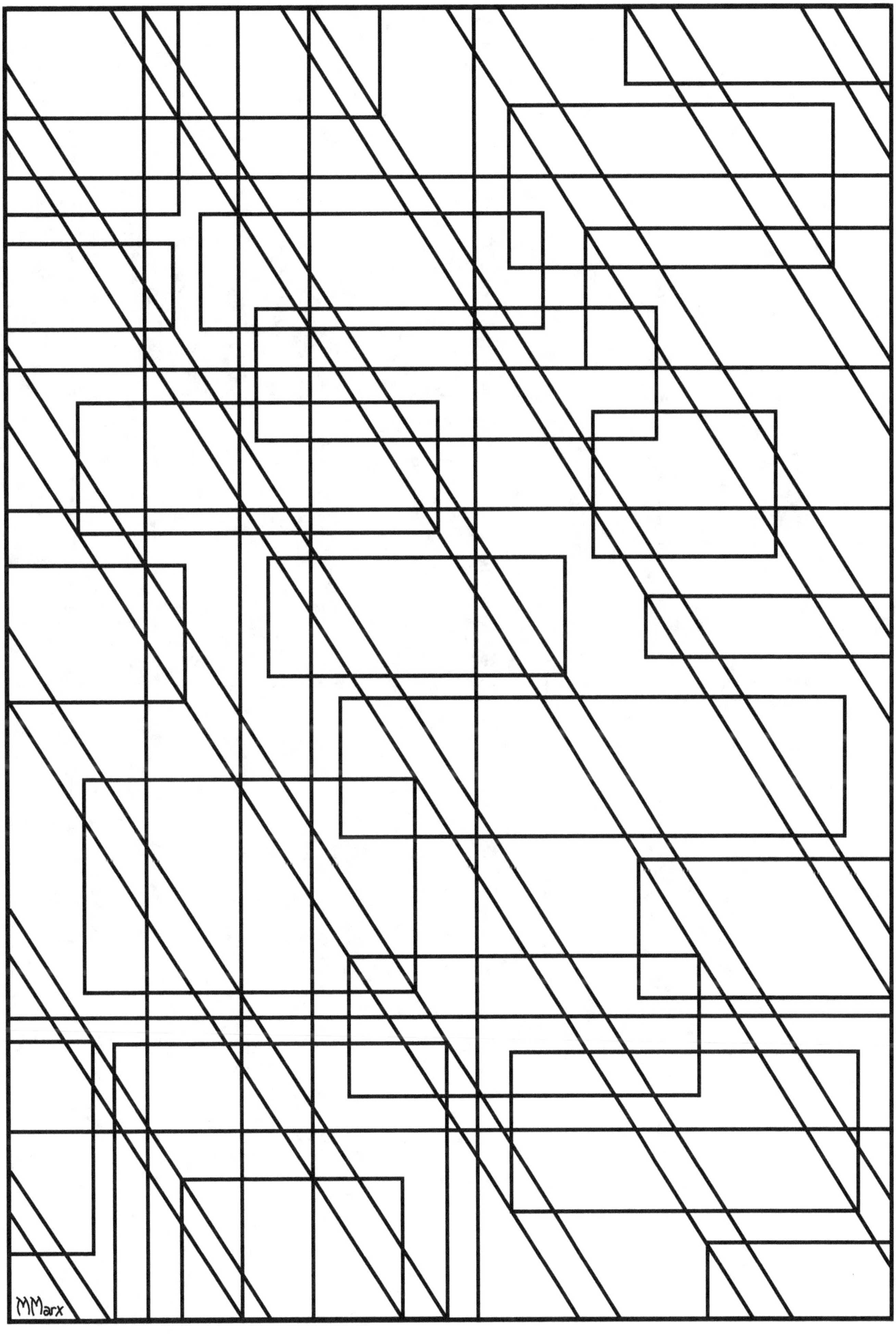
MMarx

MMarx

MMarx

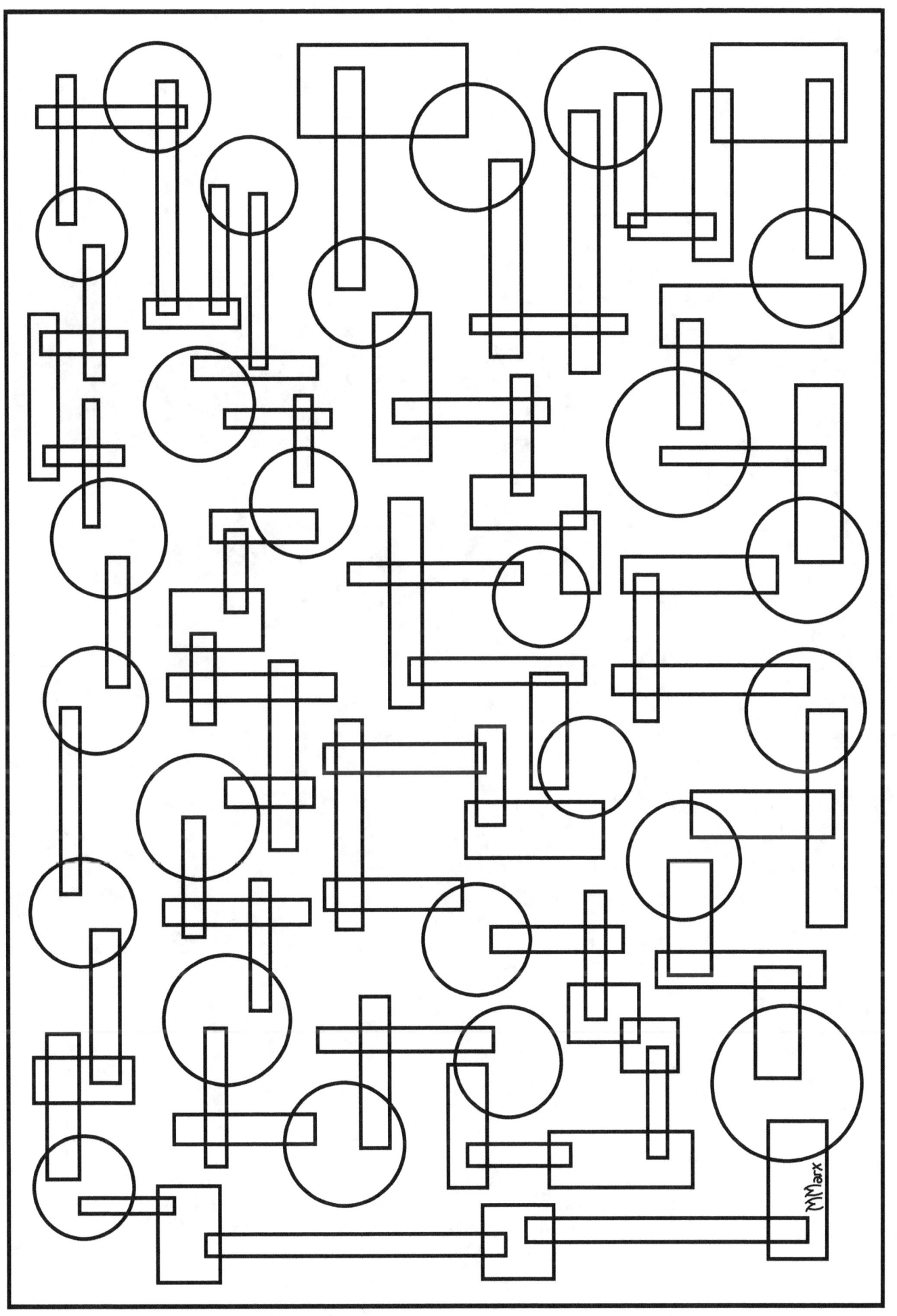

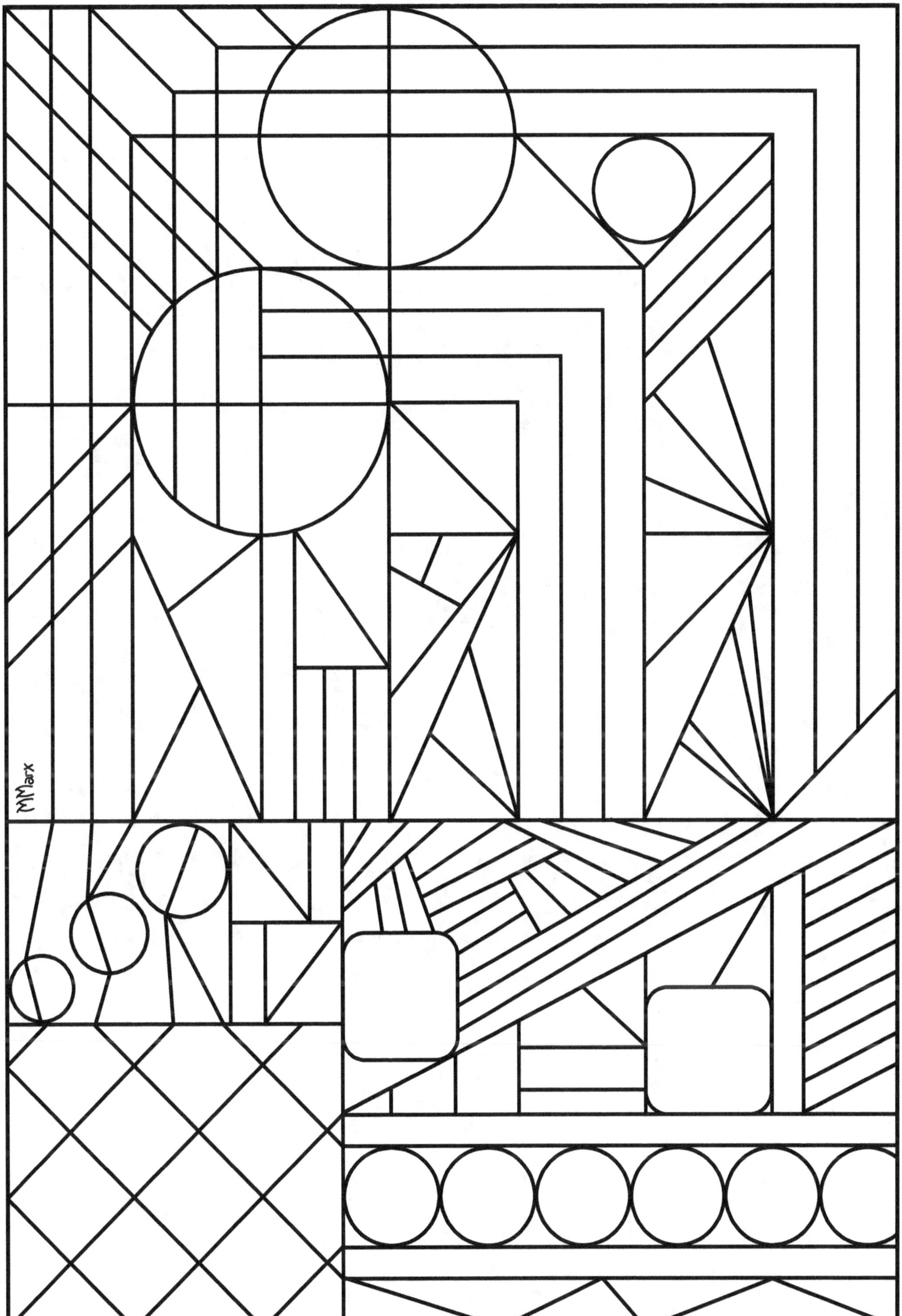
MMarx

MMarx

MMarx

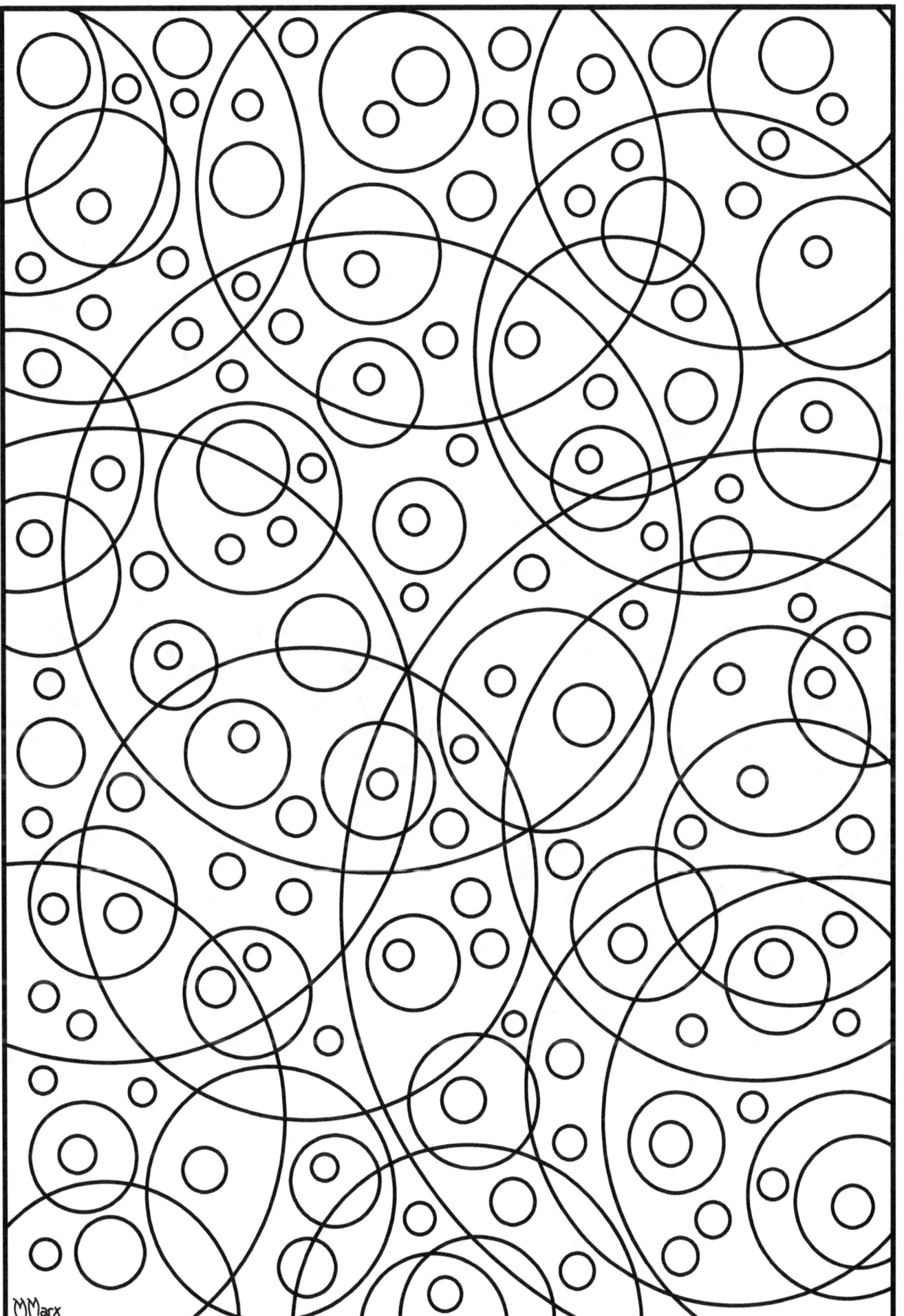

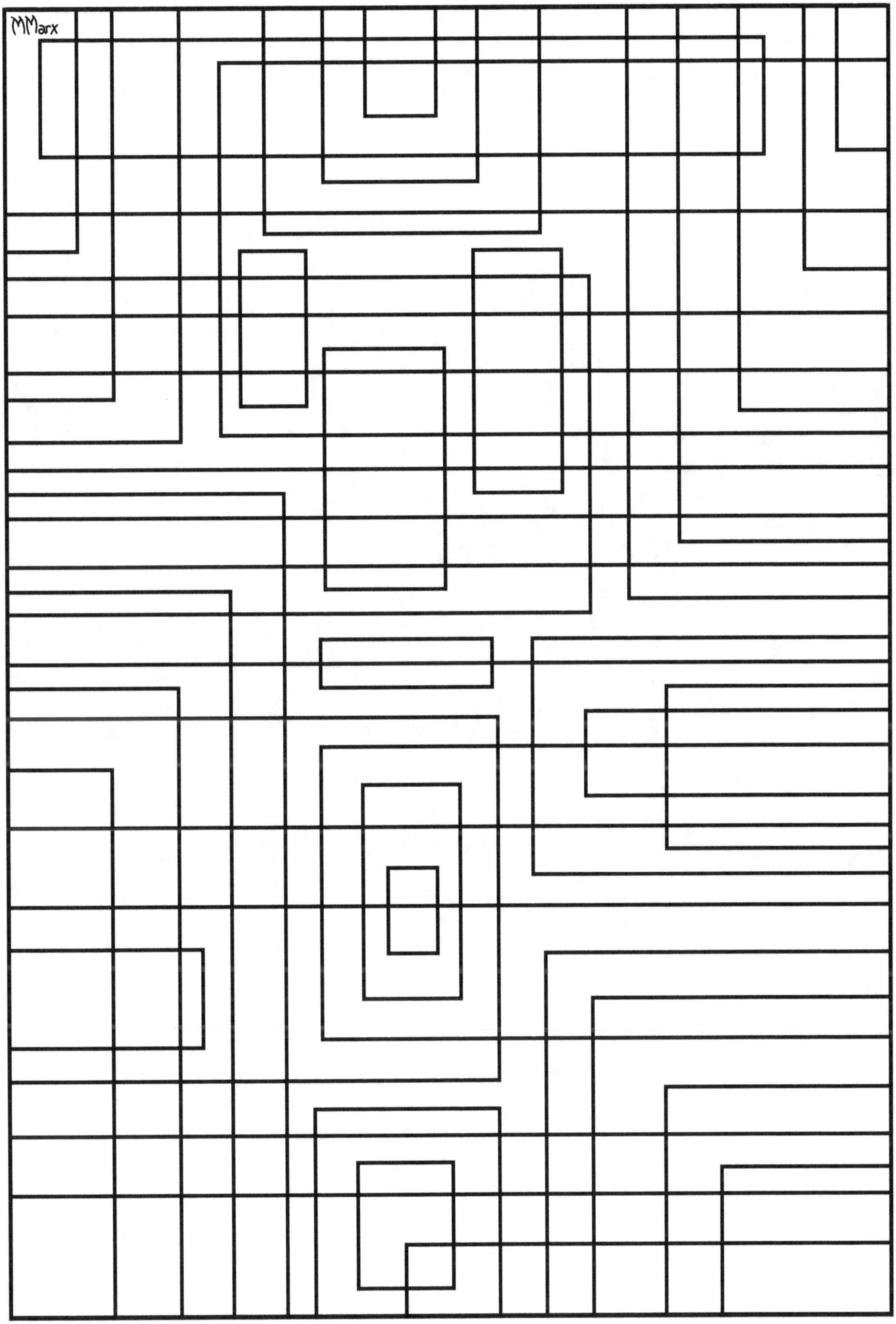
MMarx

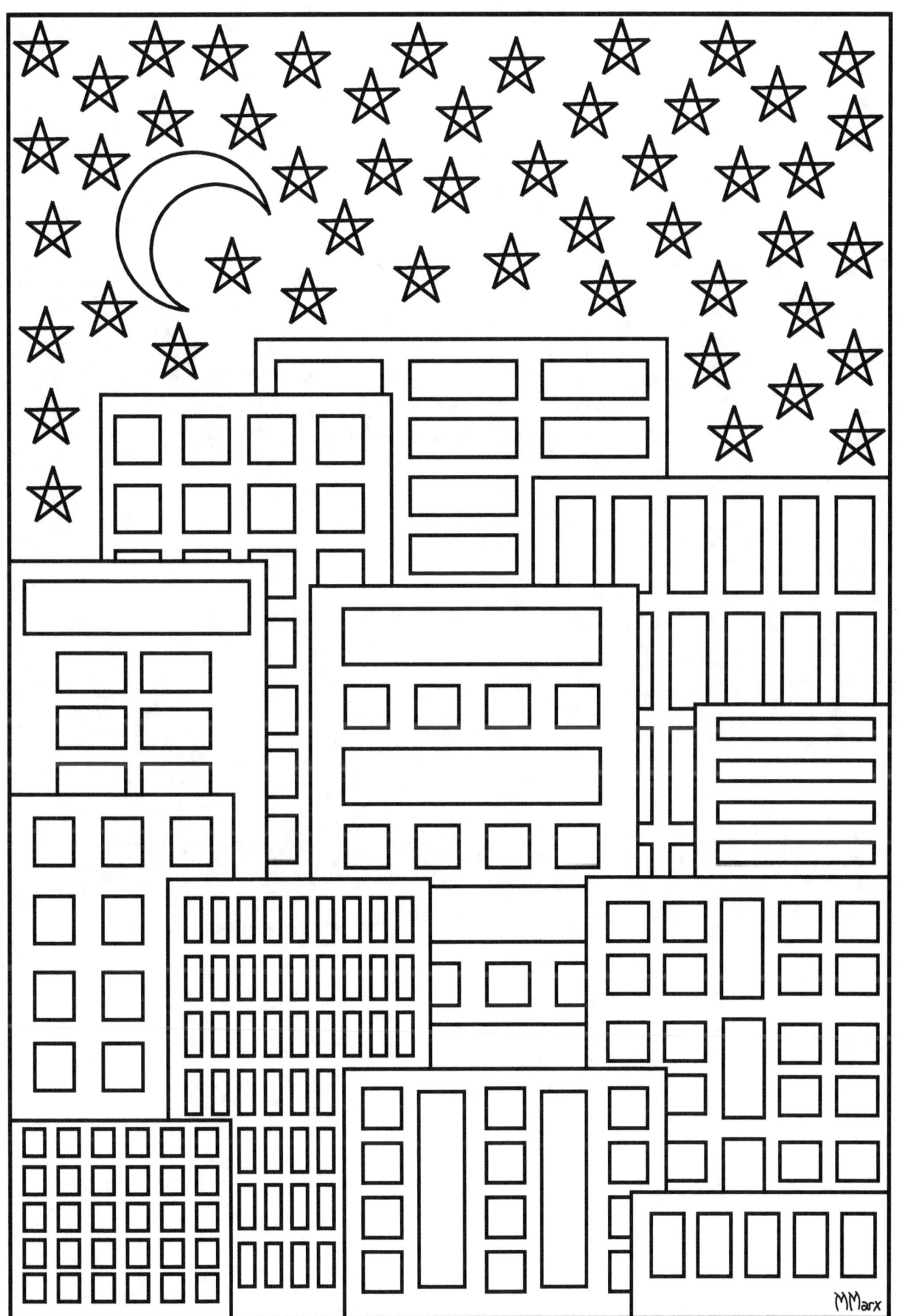

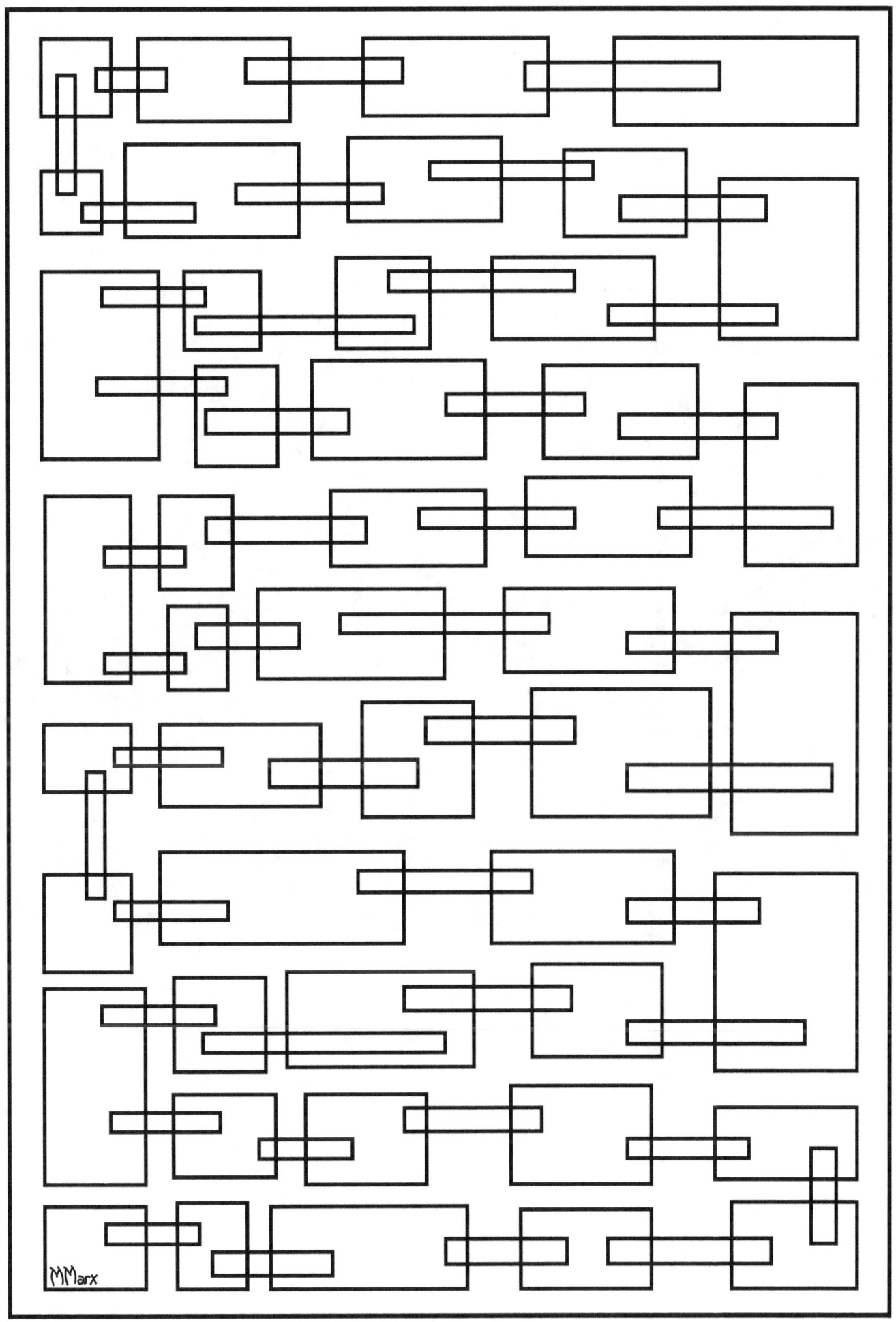

MMarx

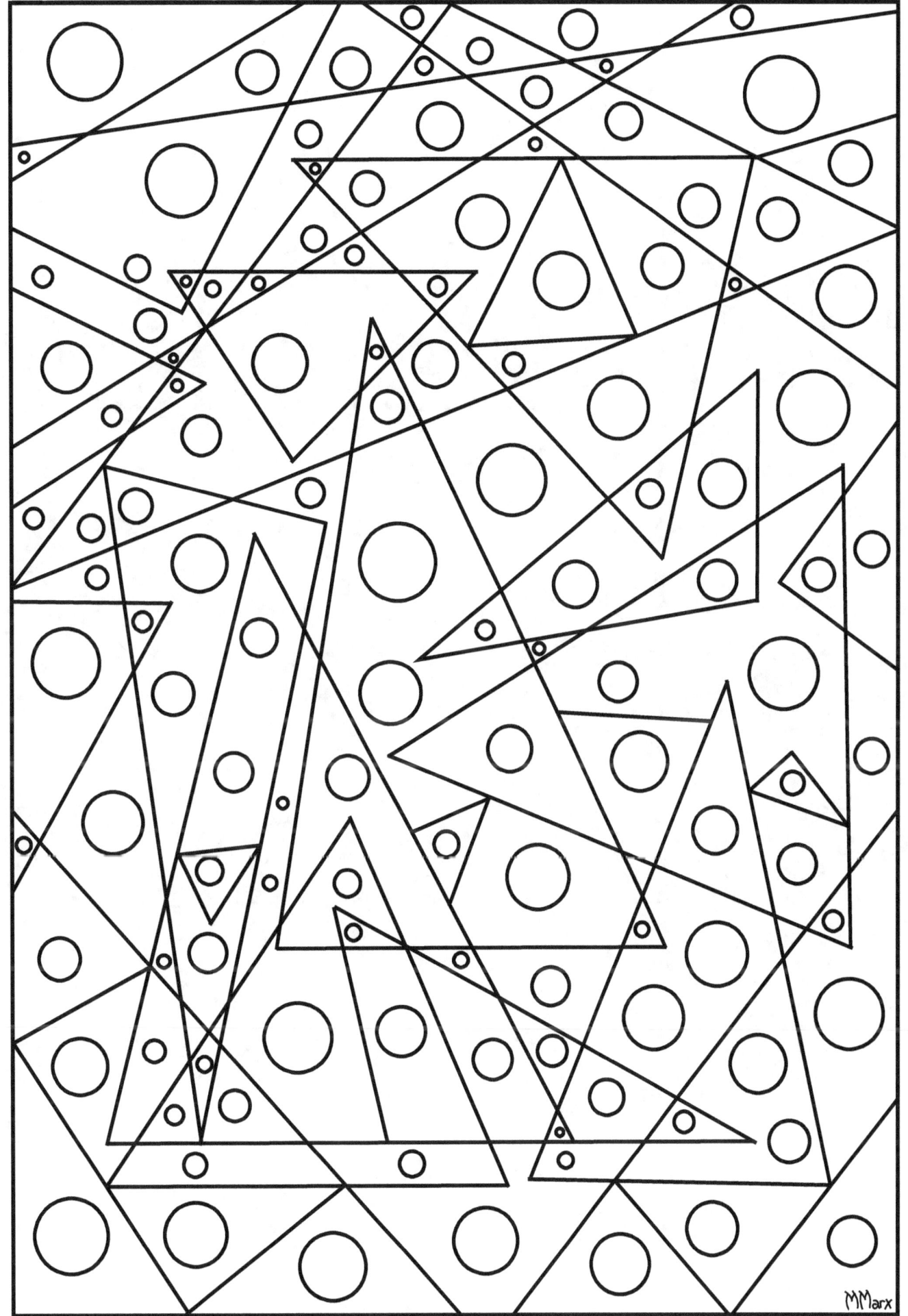

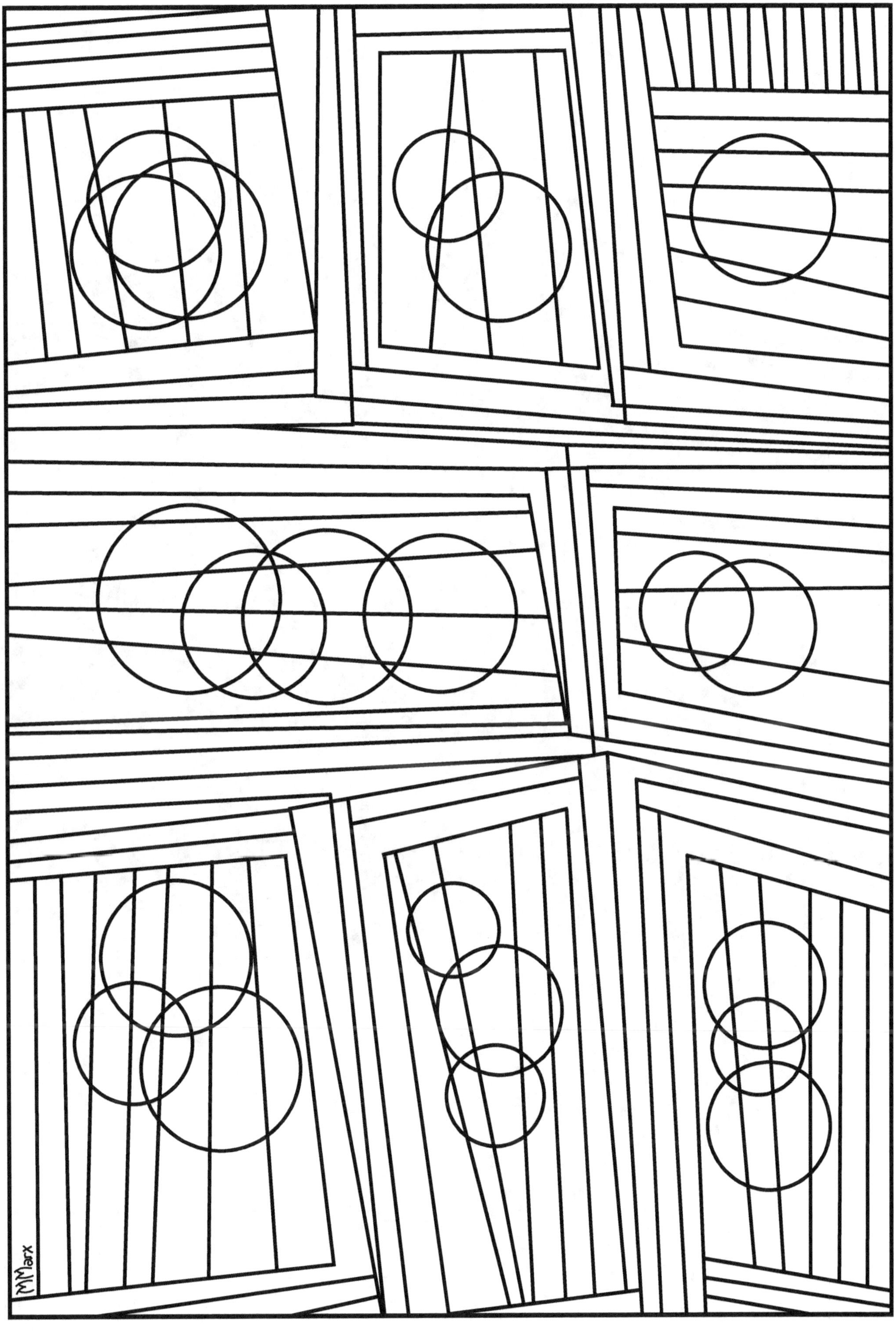
MMarx

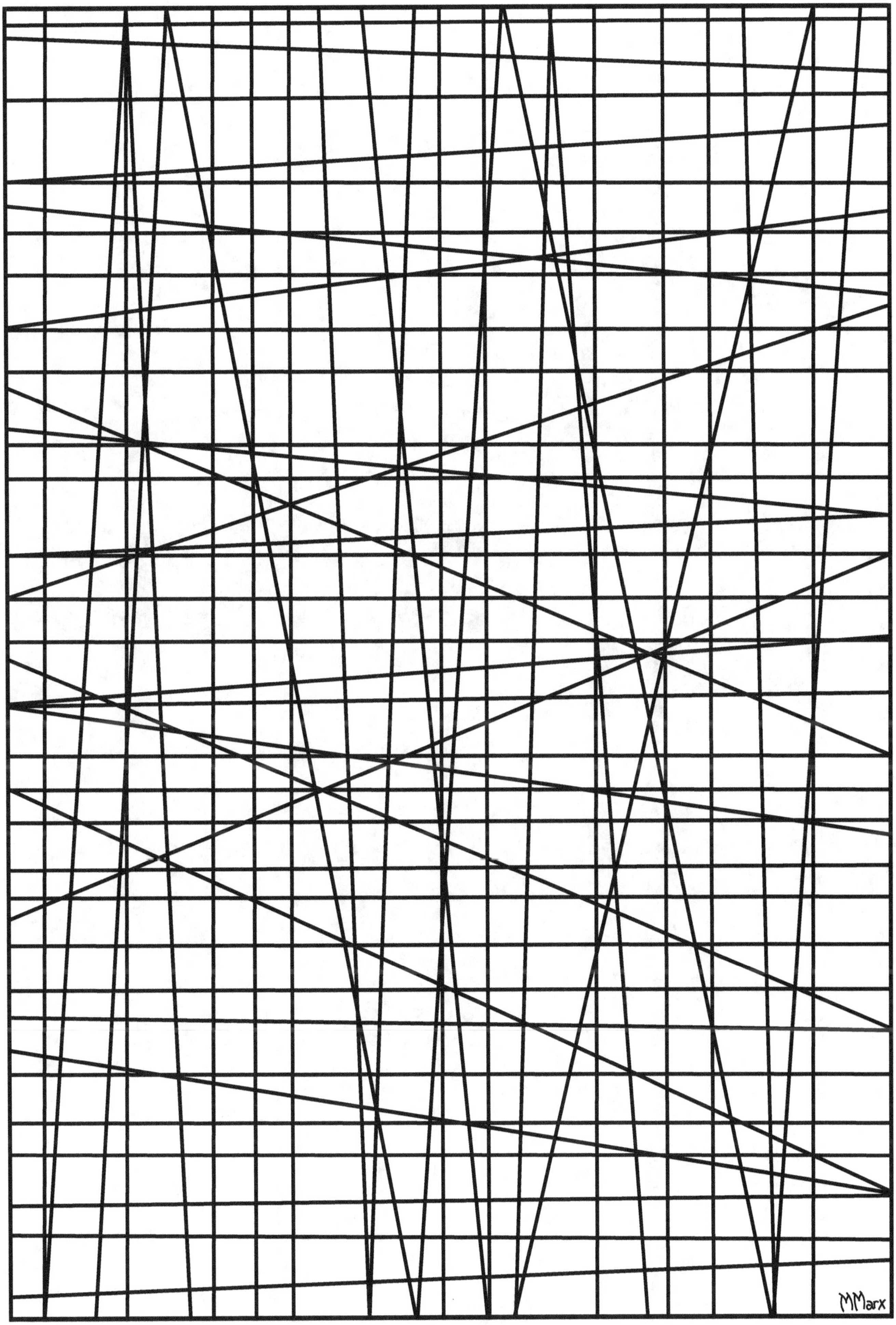
MMarx

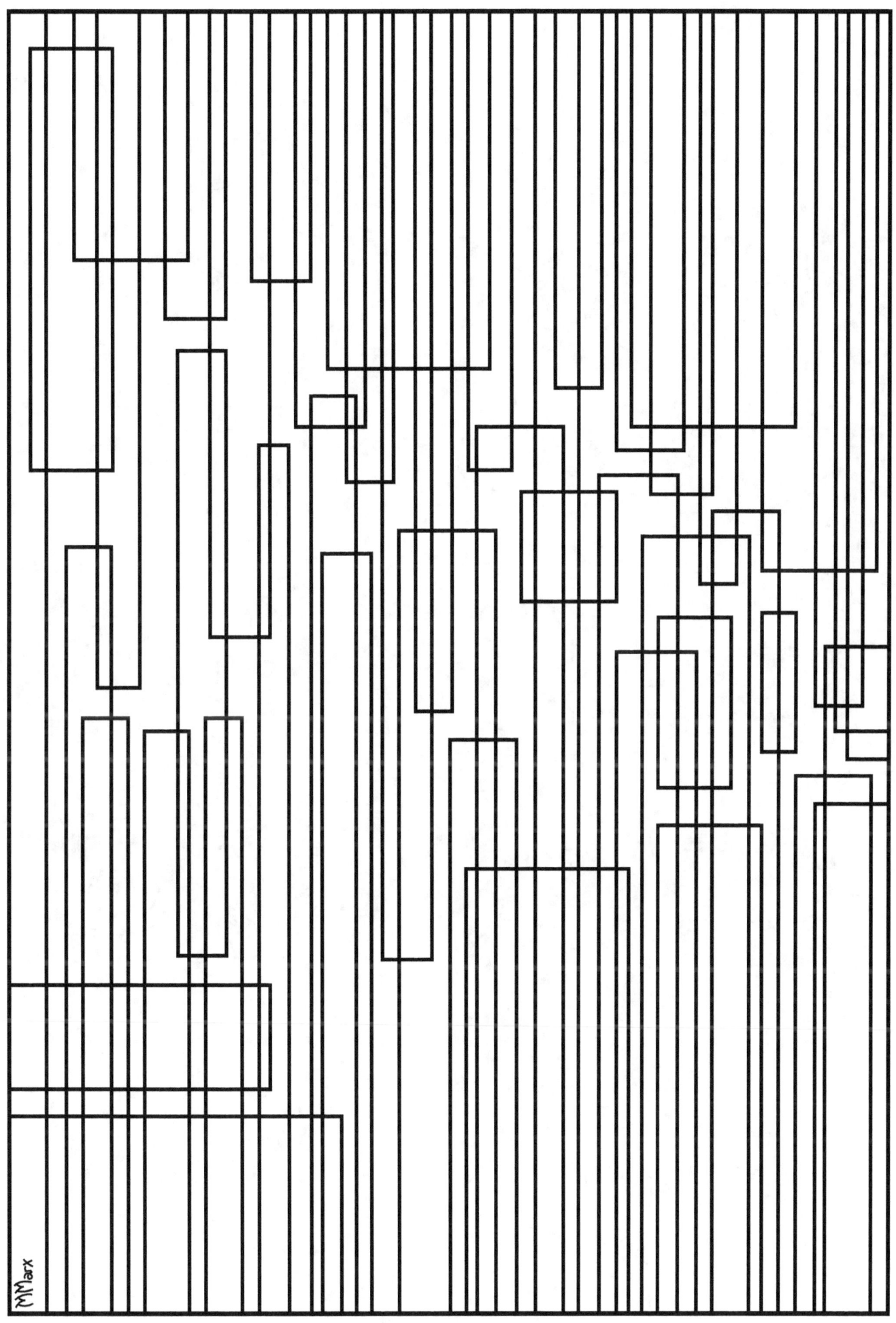

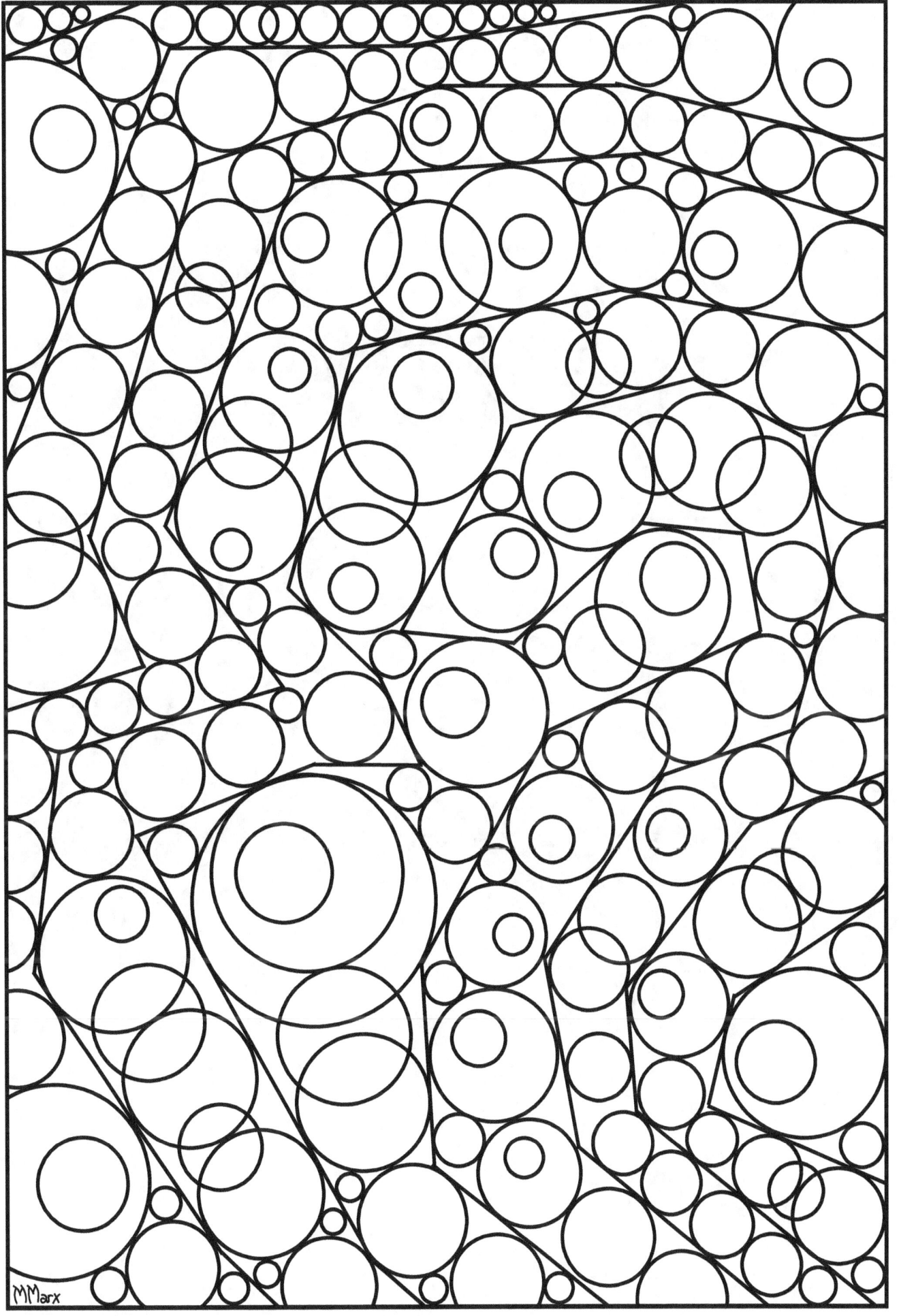

MMarx

MMarx

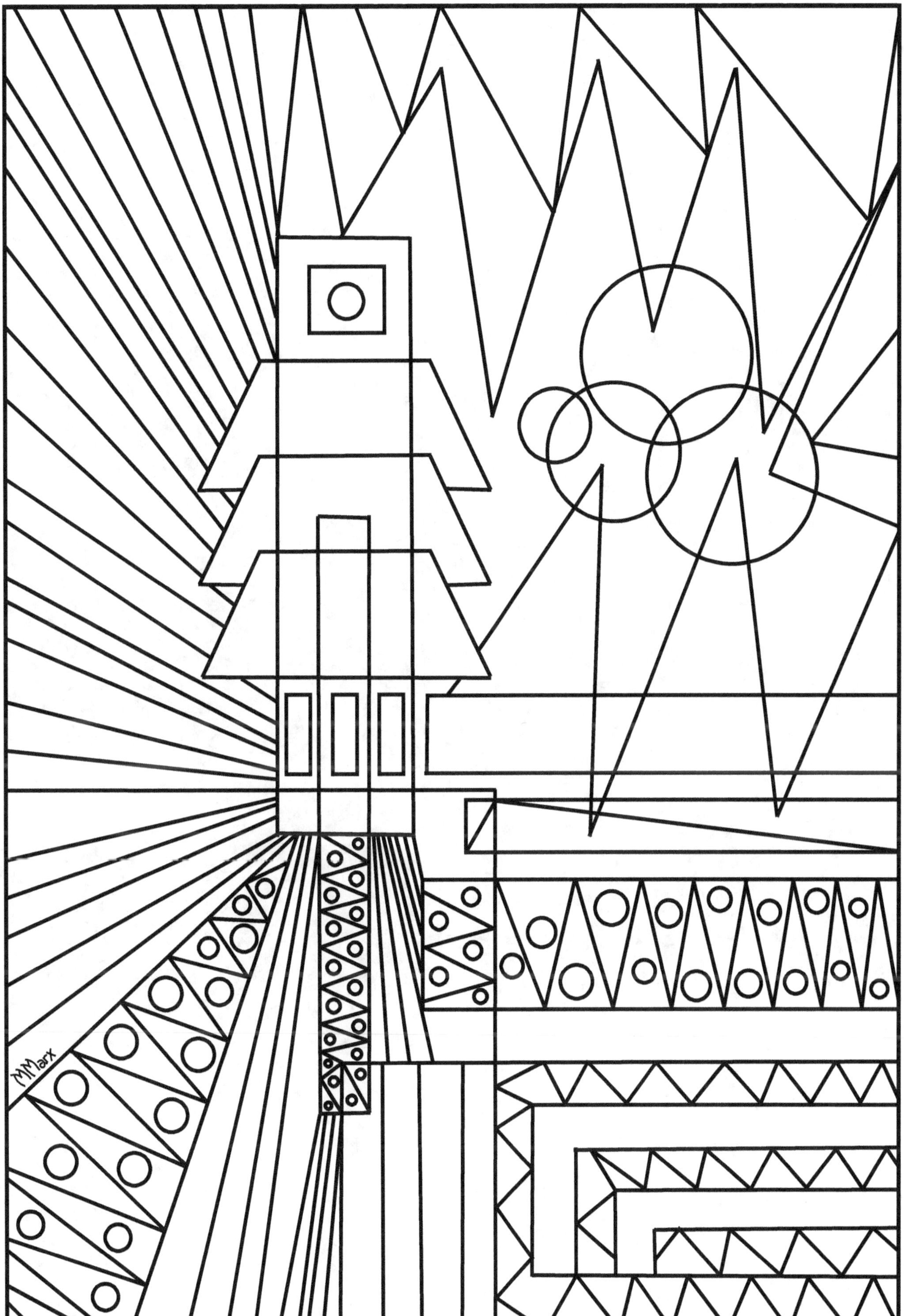
MMarx

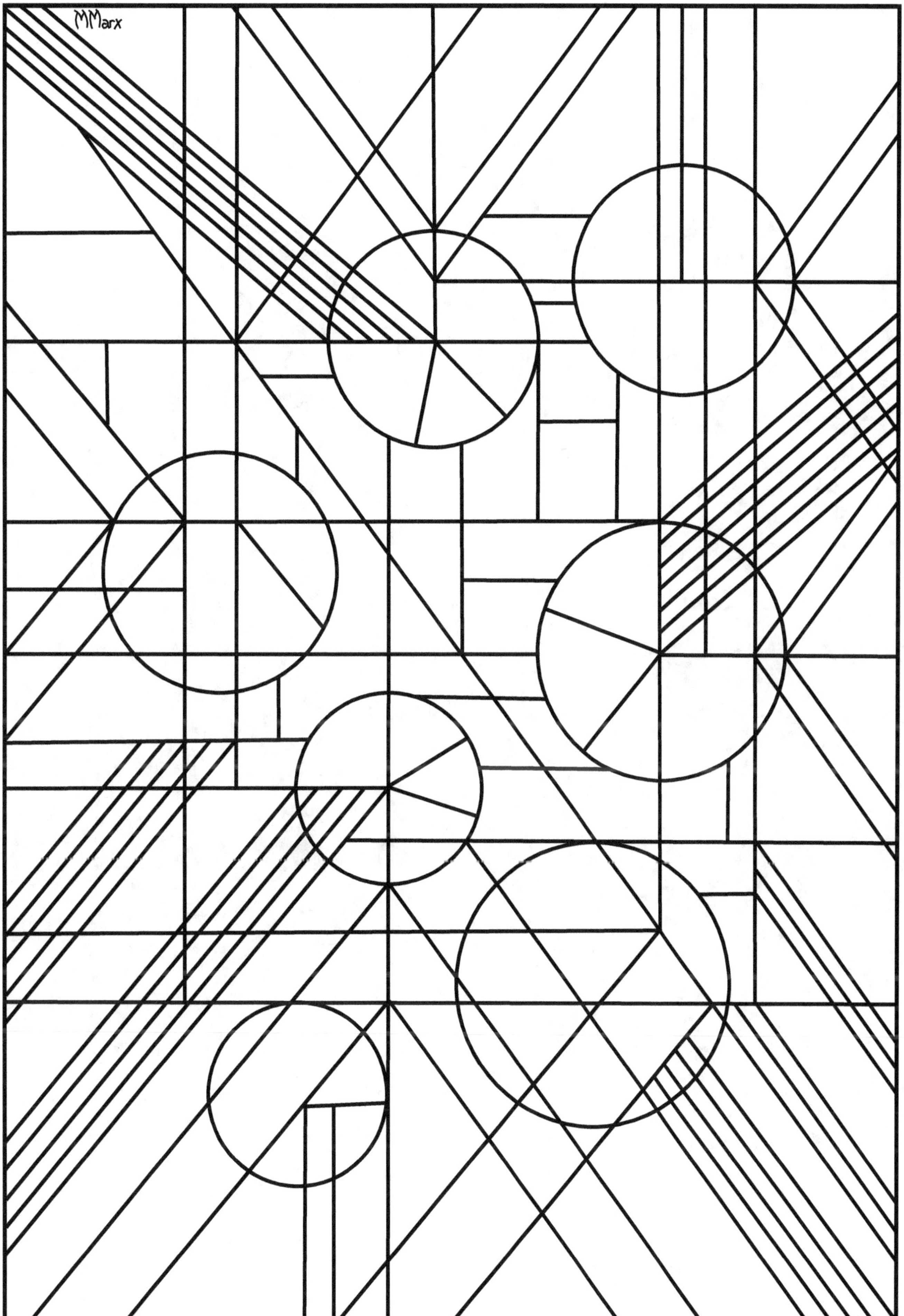
MMarx

MMarx

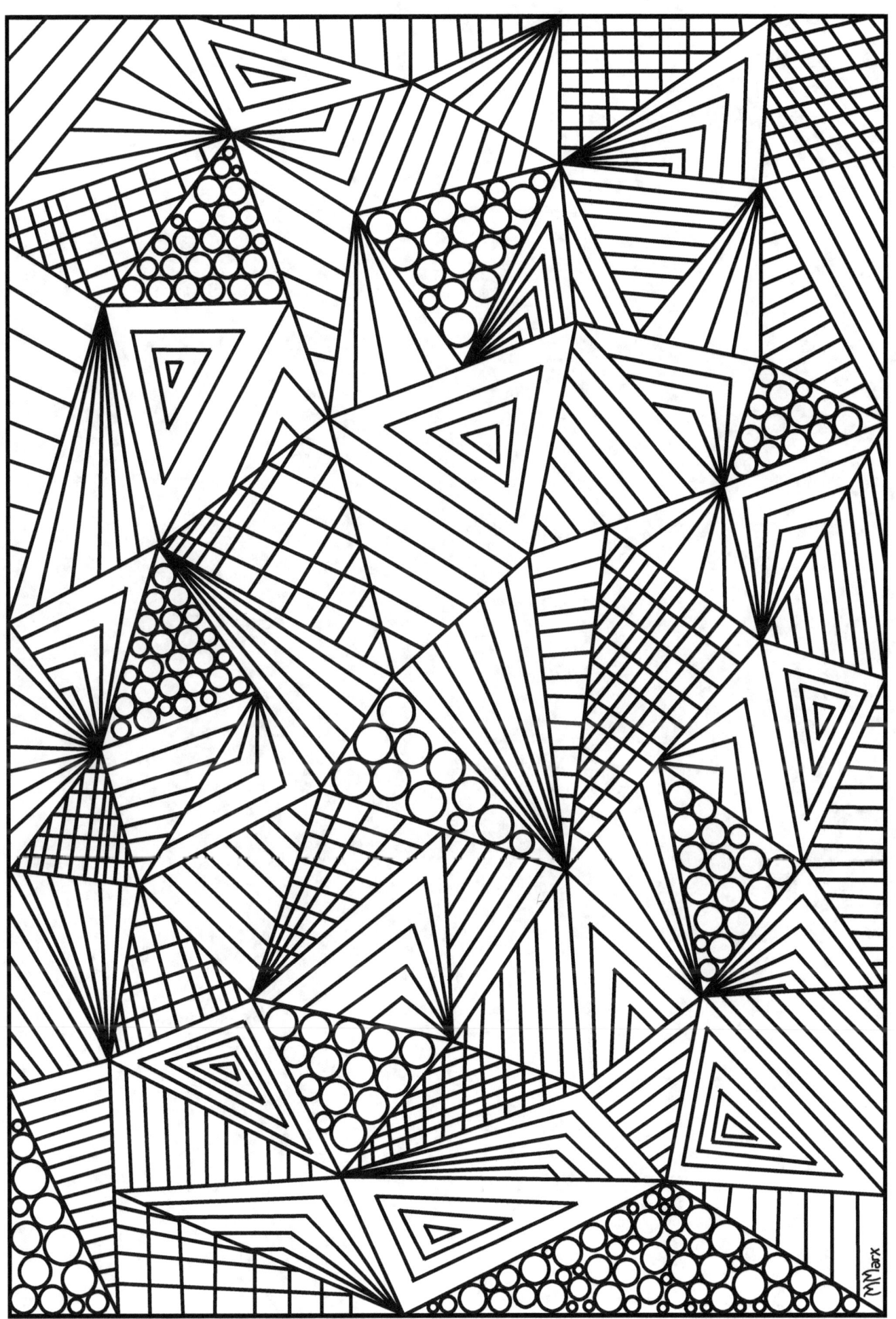

MMarx

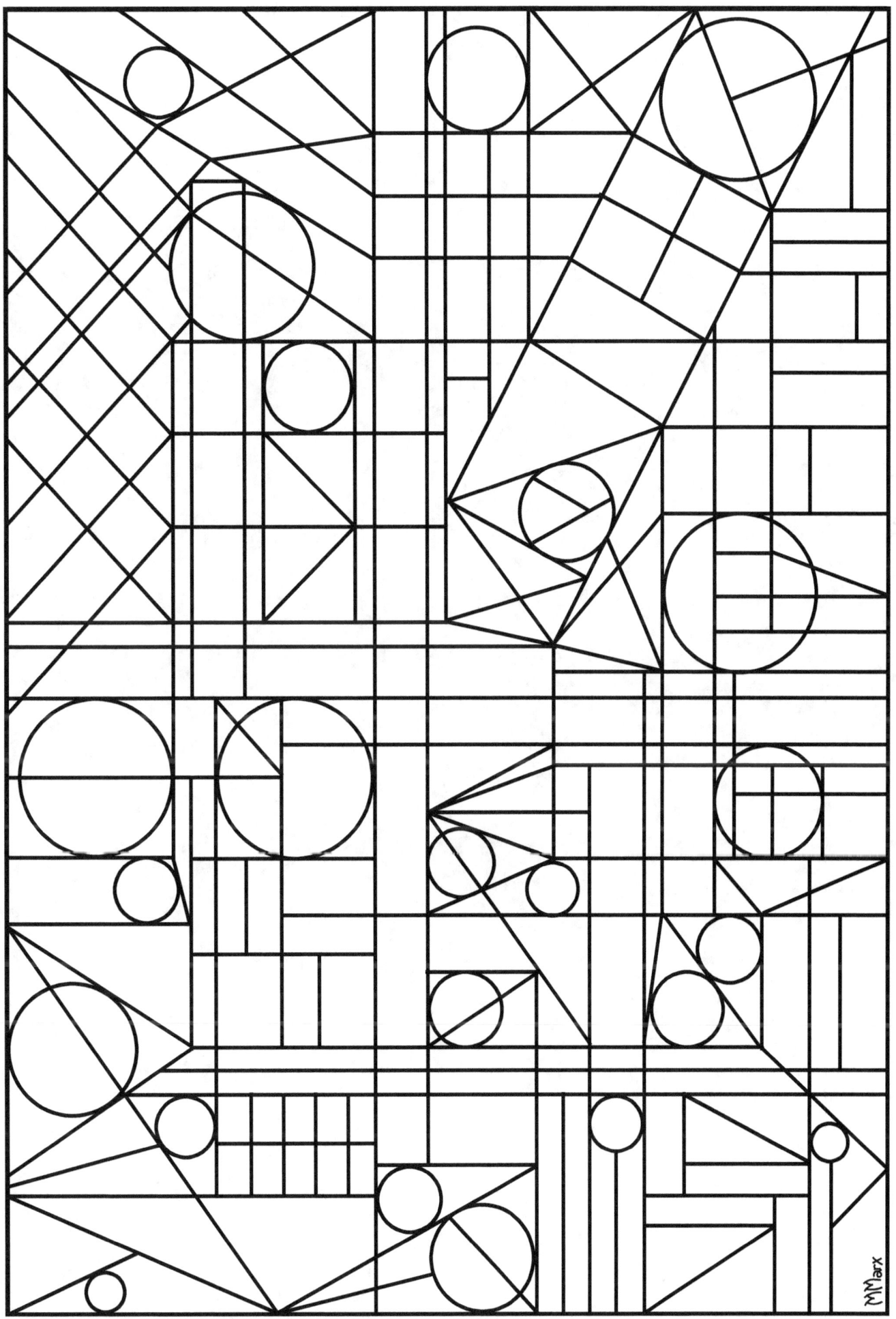

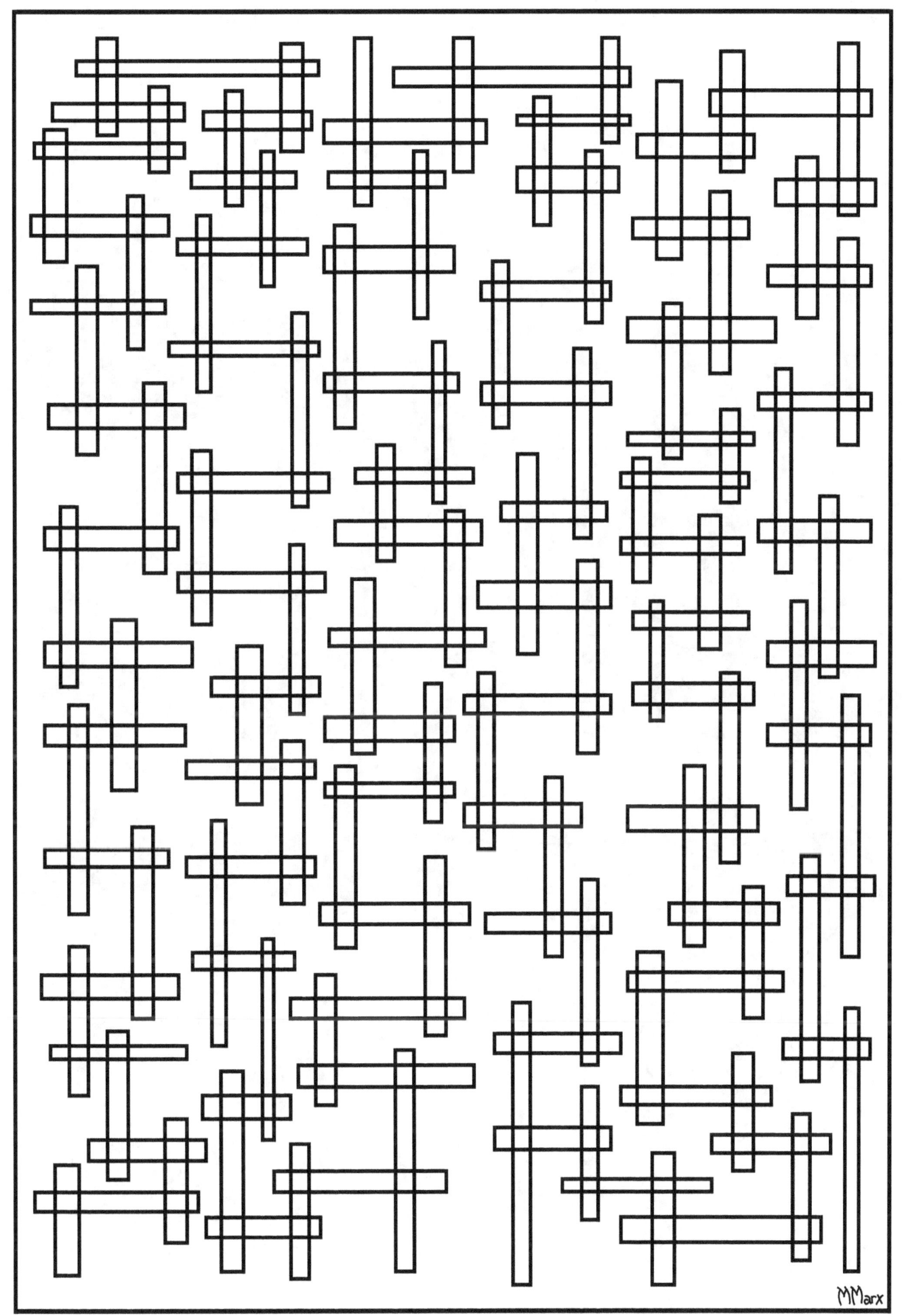

MMarx

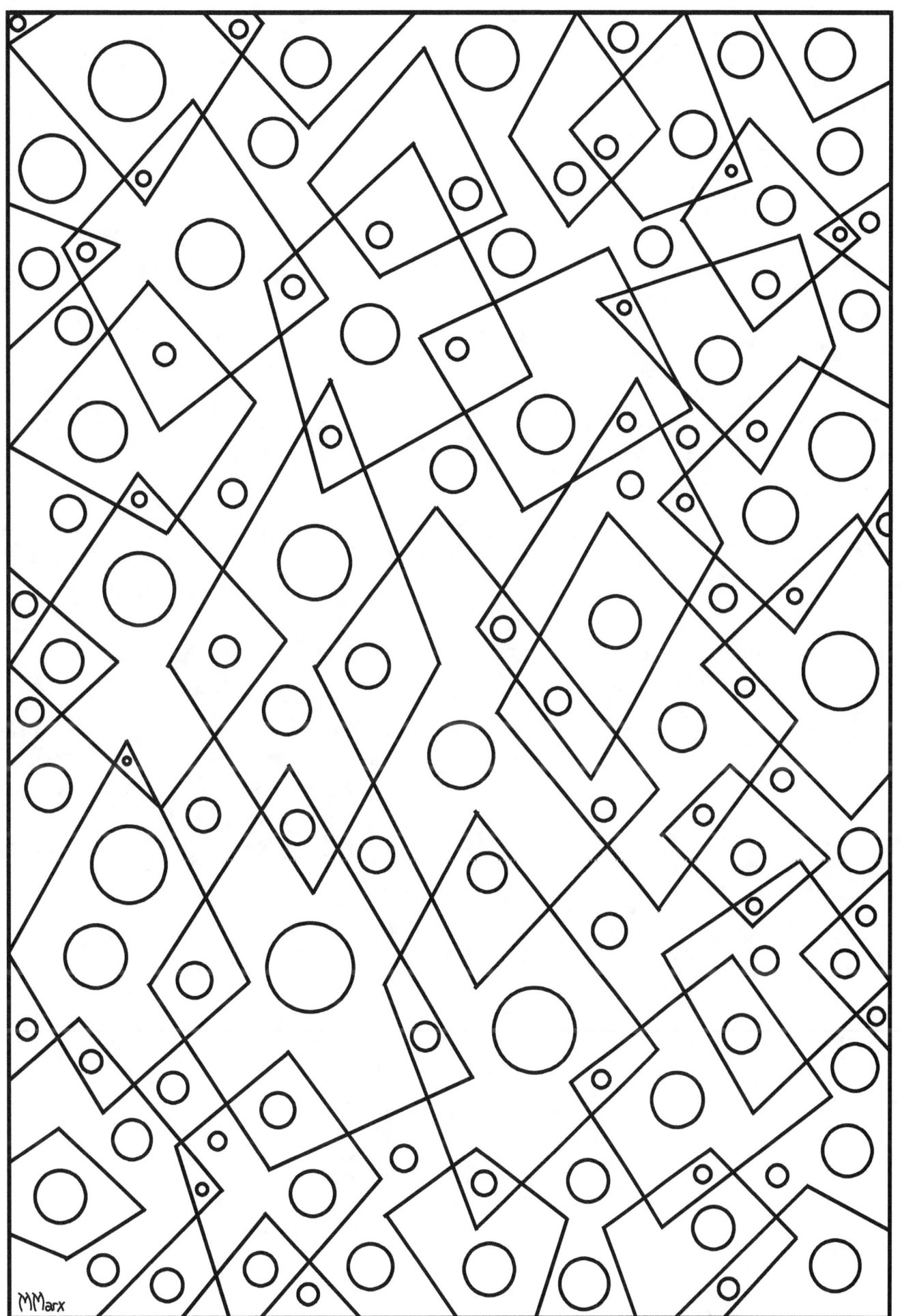

MMarx

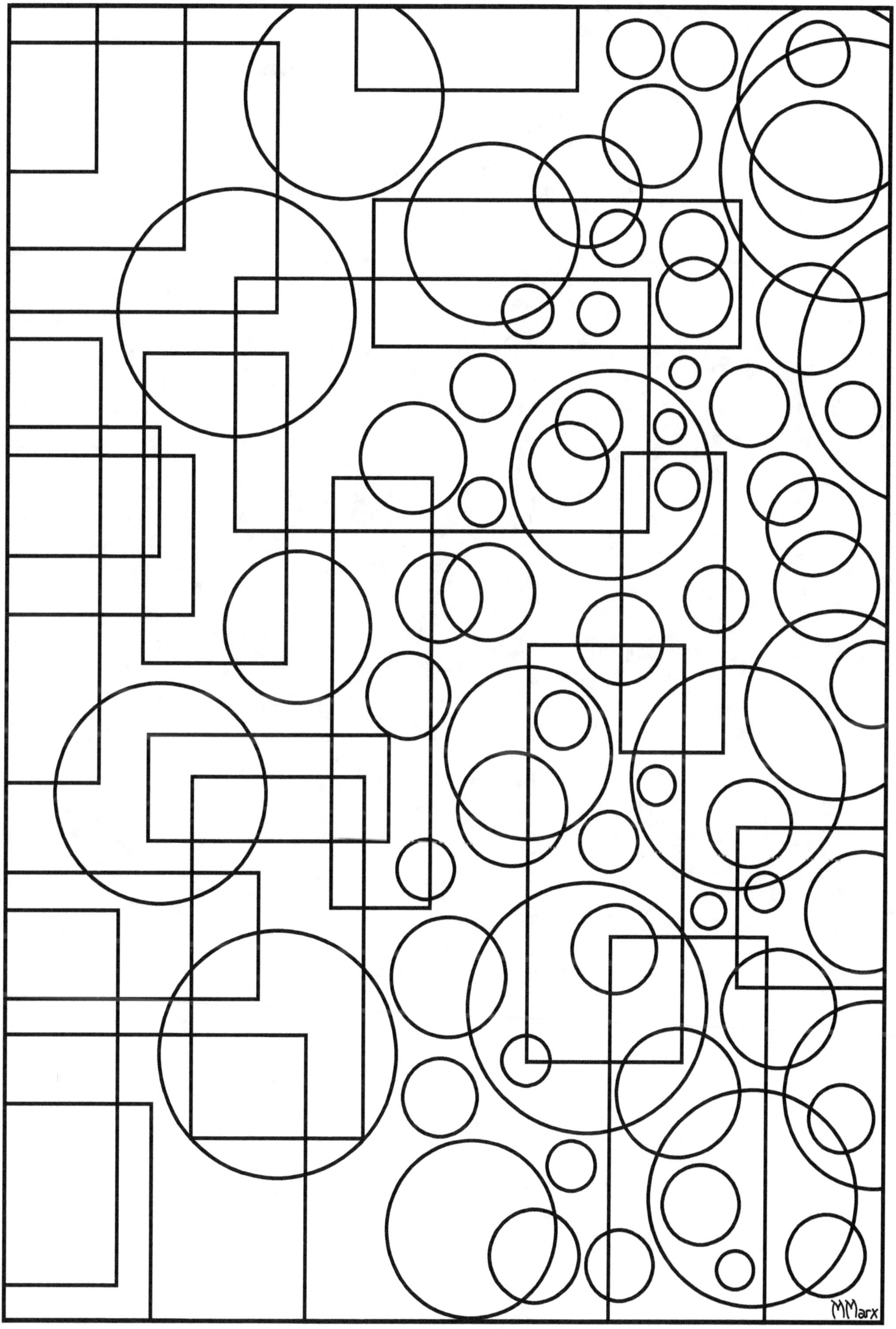
MMarx

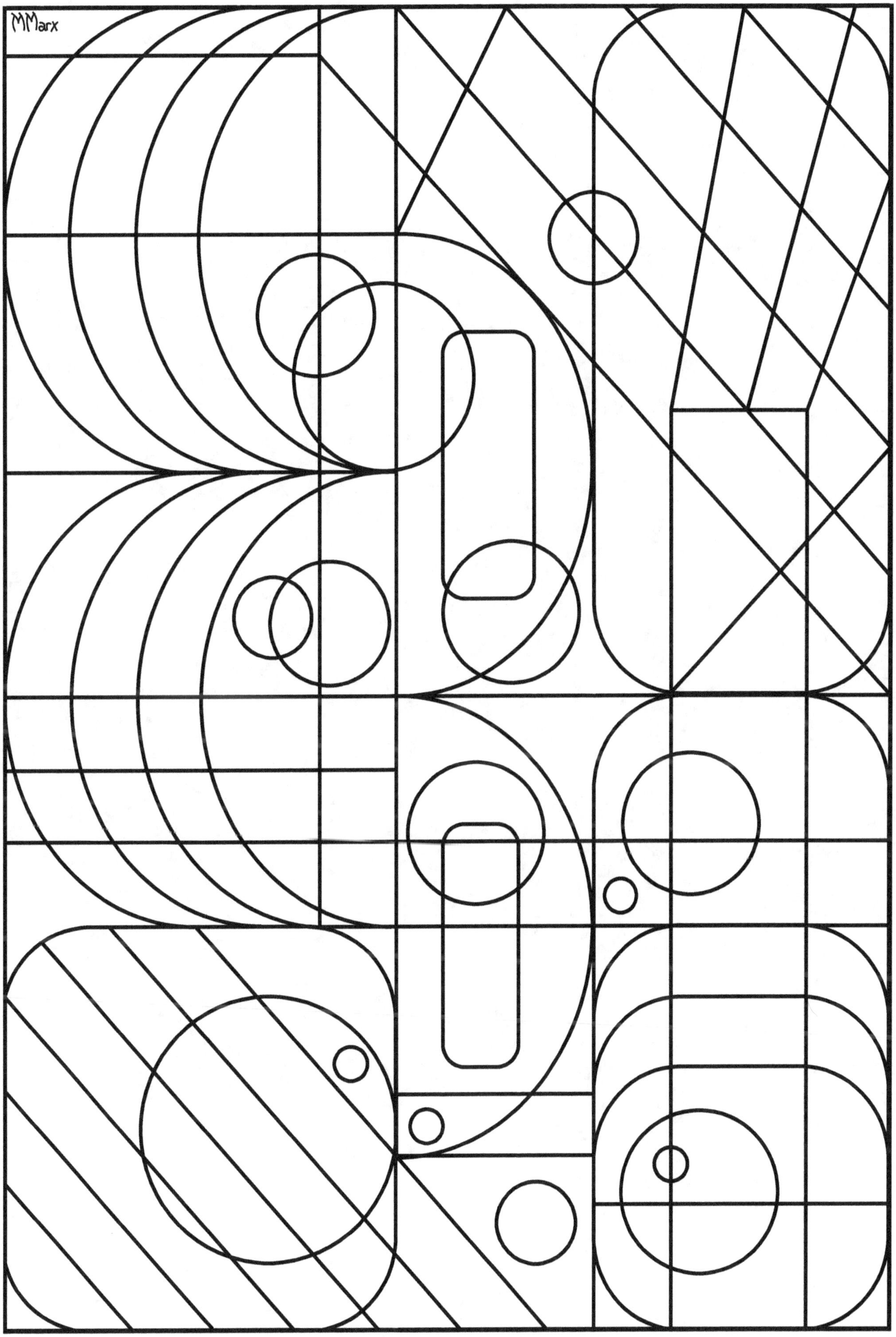
MMarx

MMarx

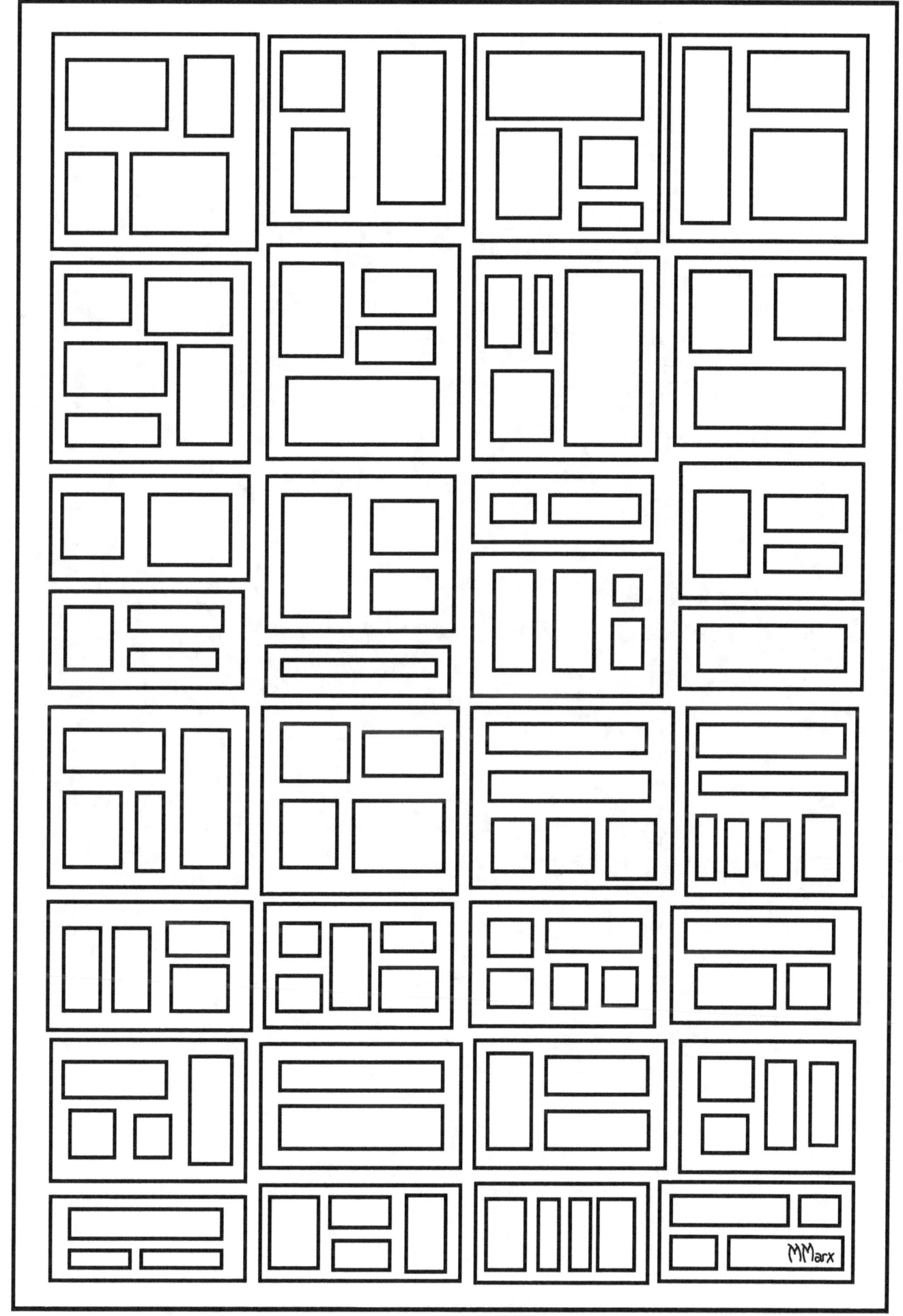

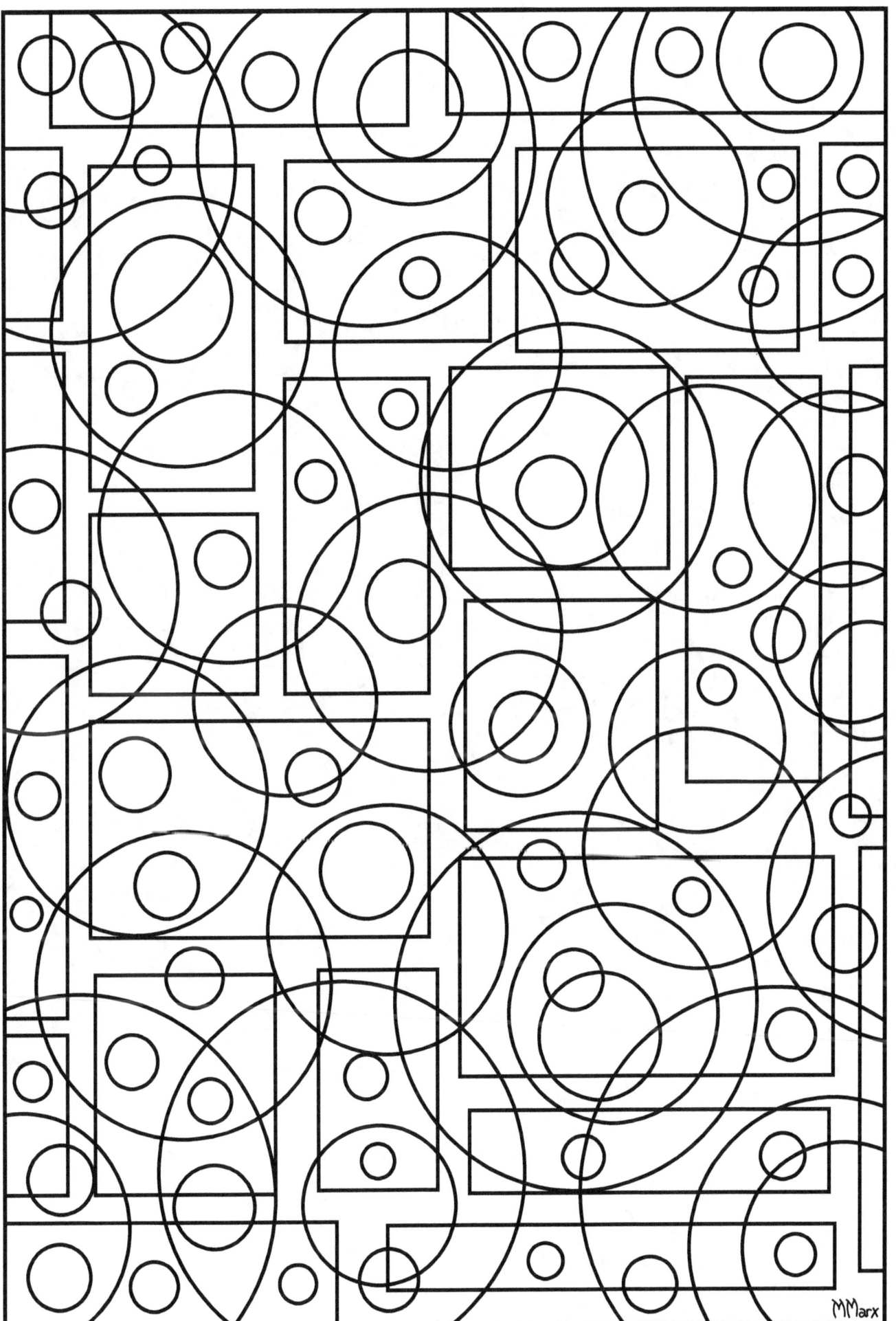

MMarx

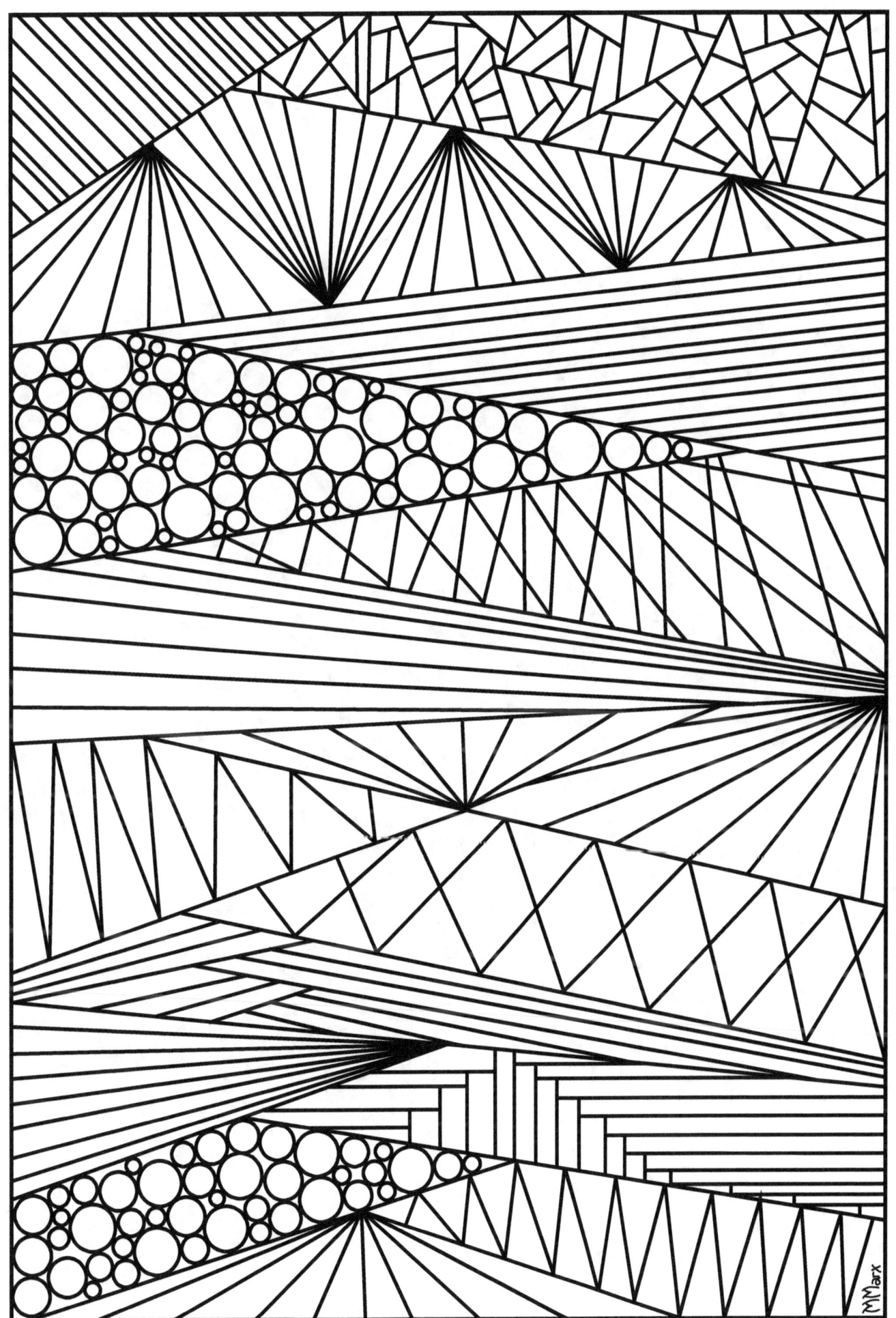

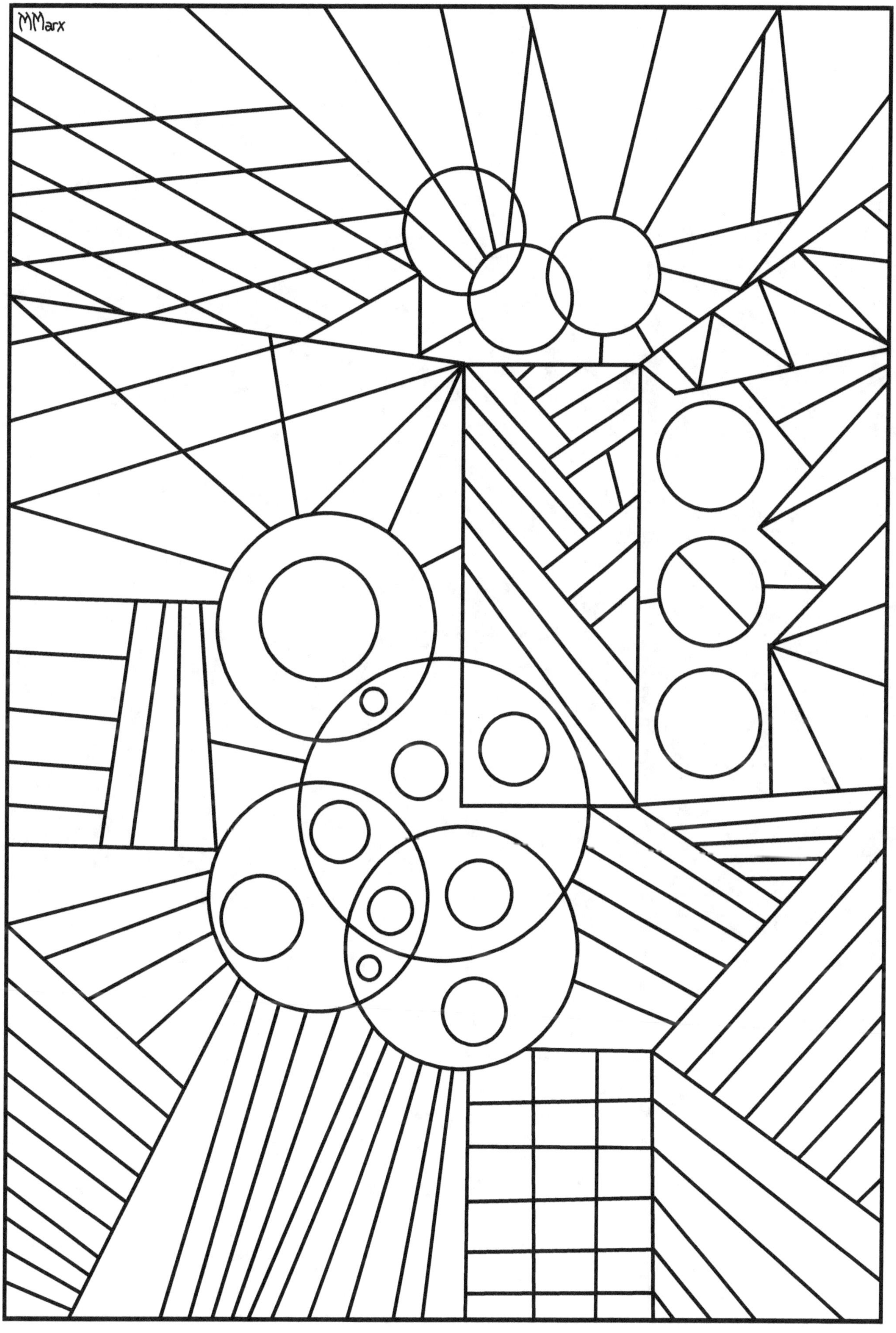
MMarx

MMarx

MMarx

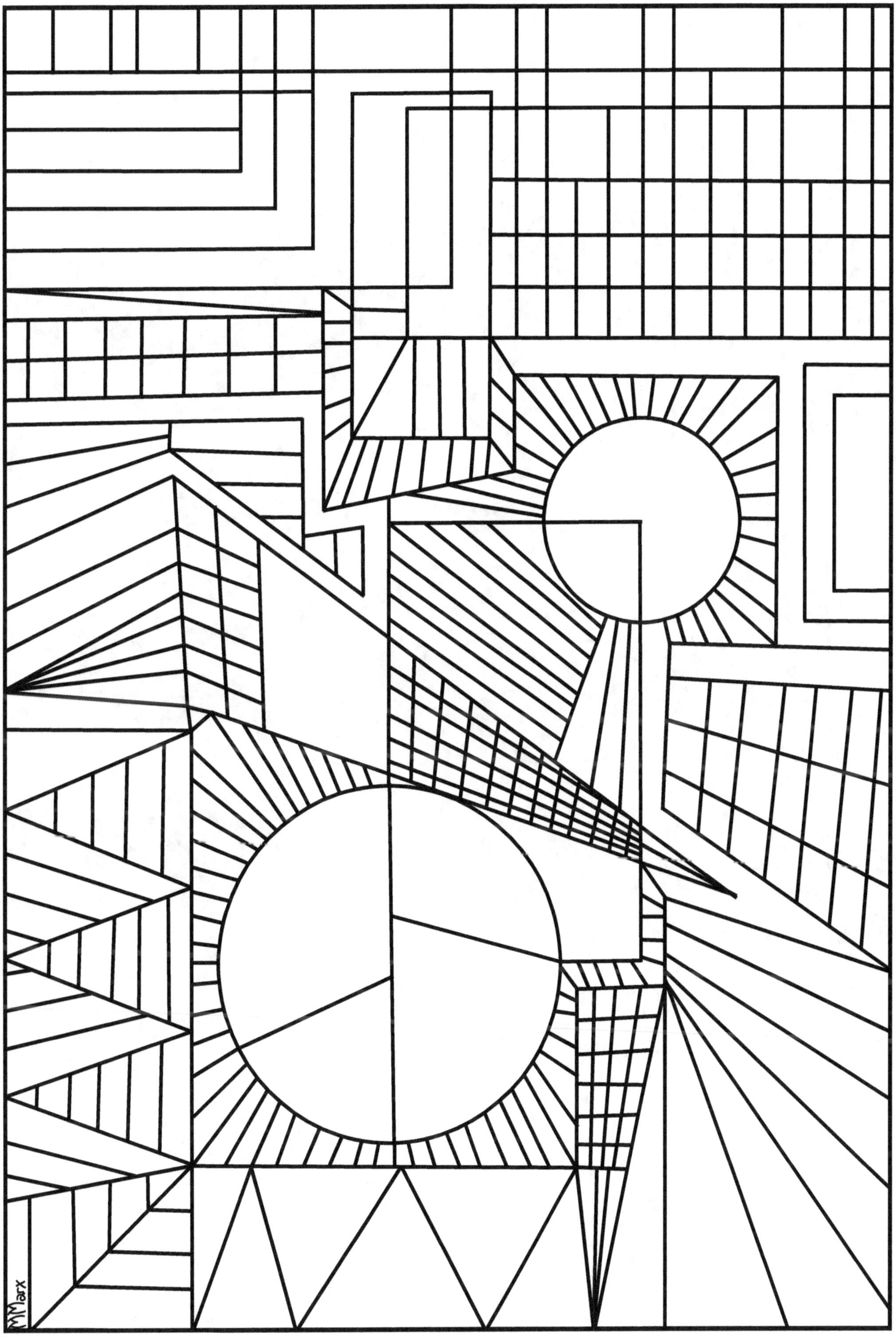
MMarx

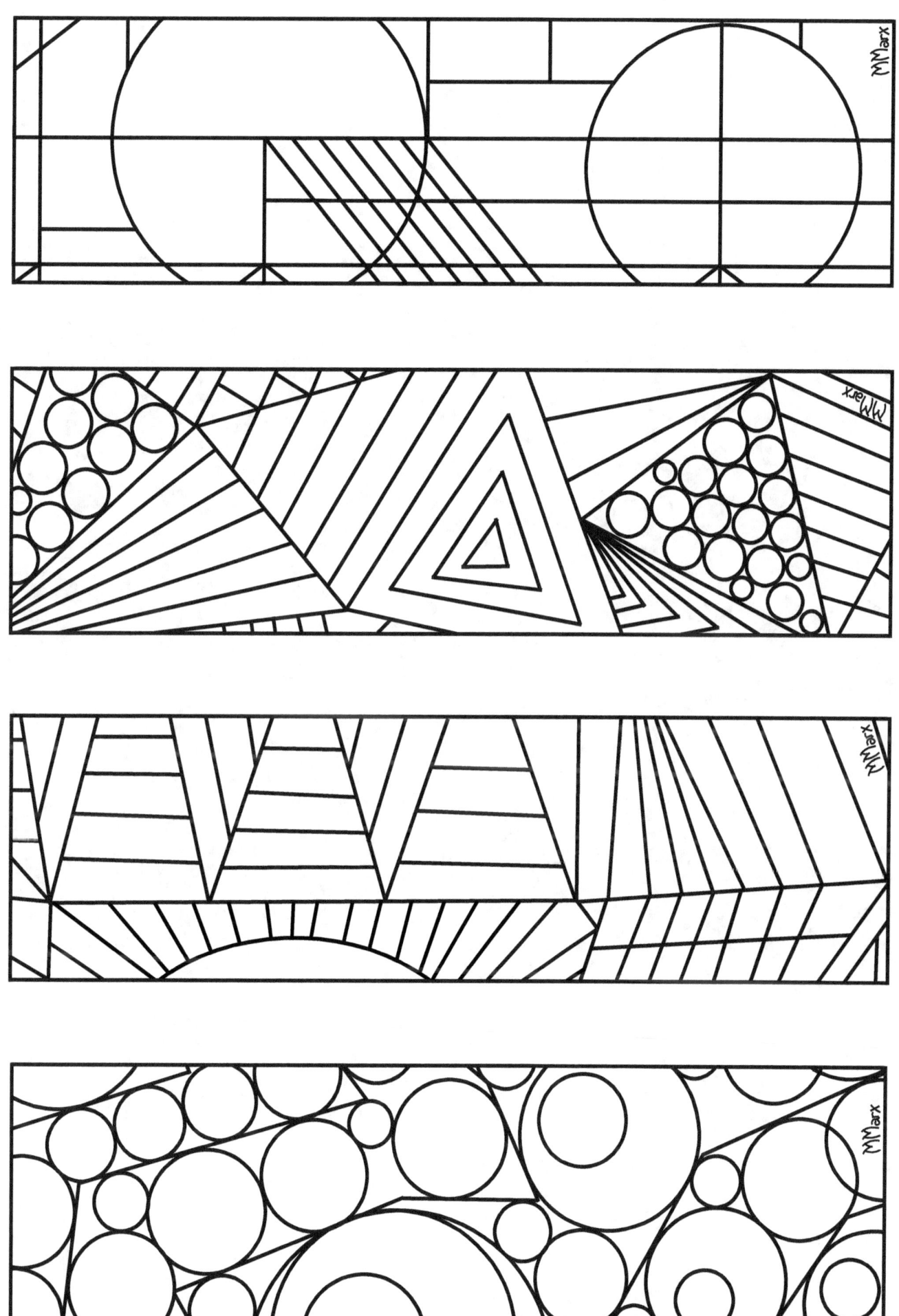

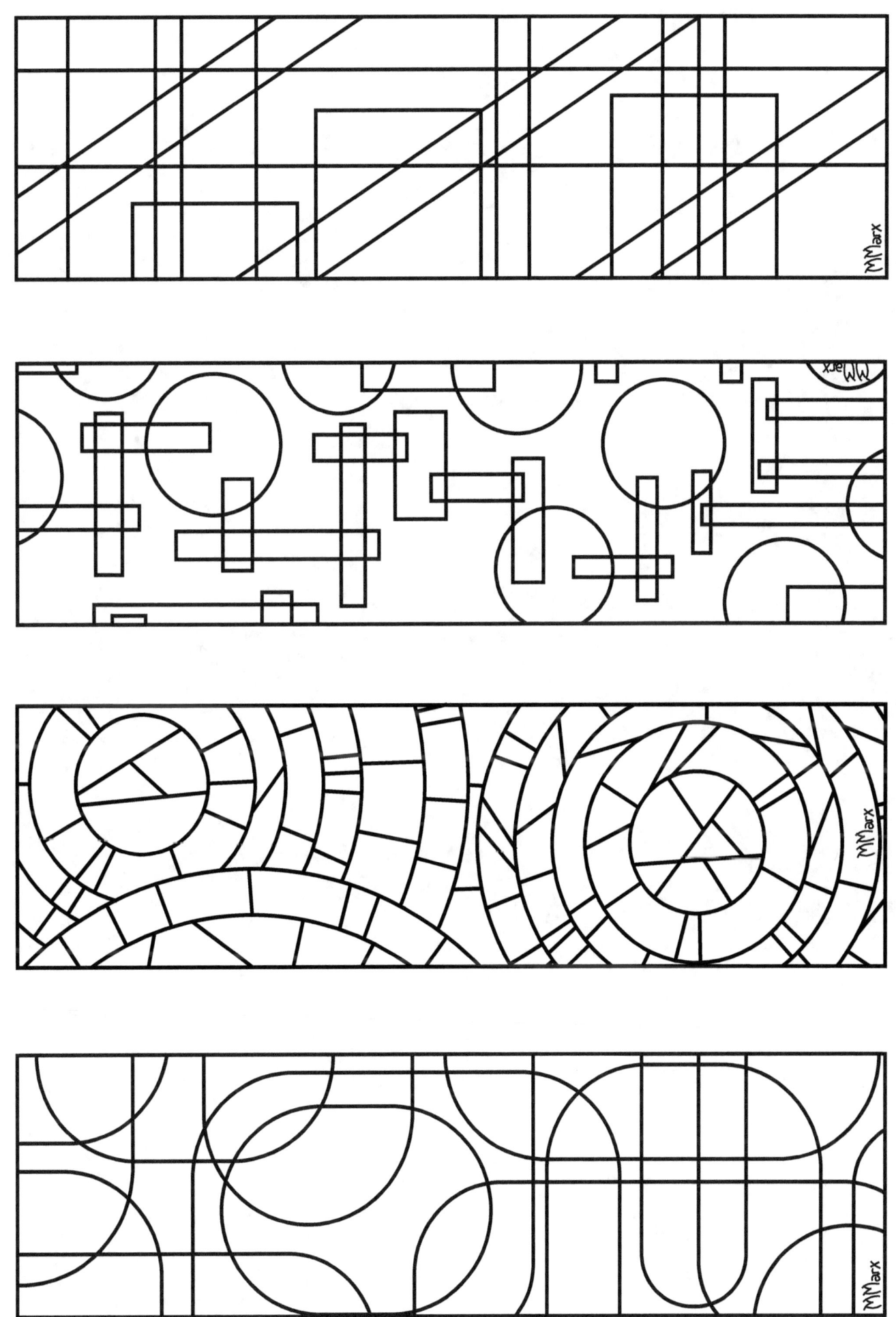

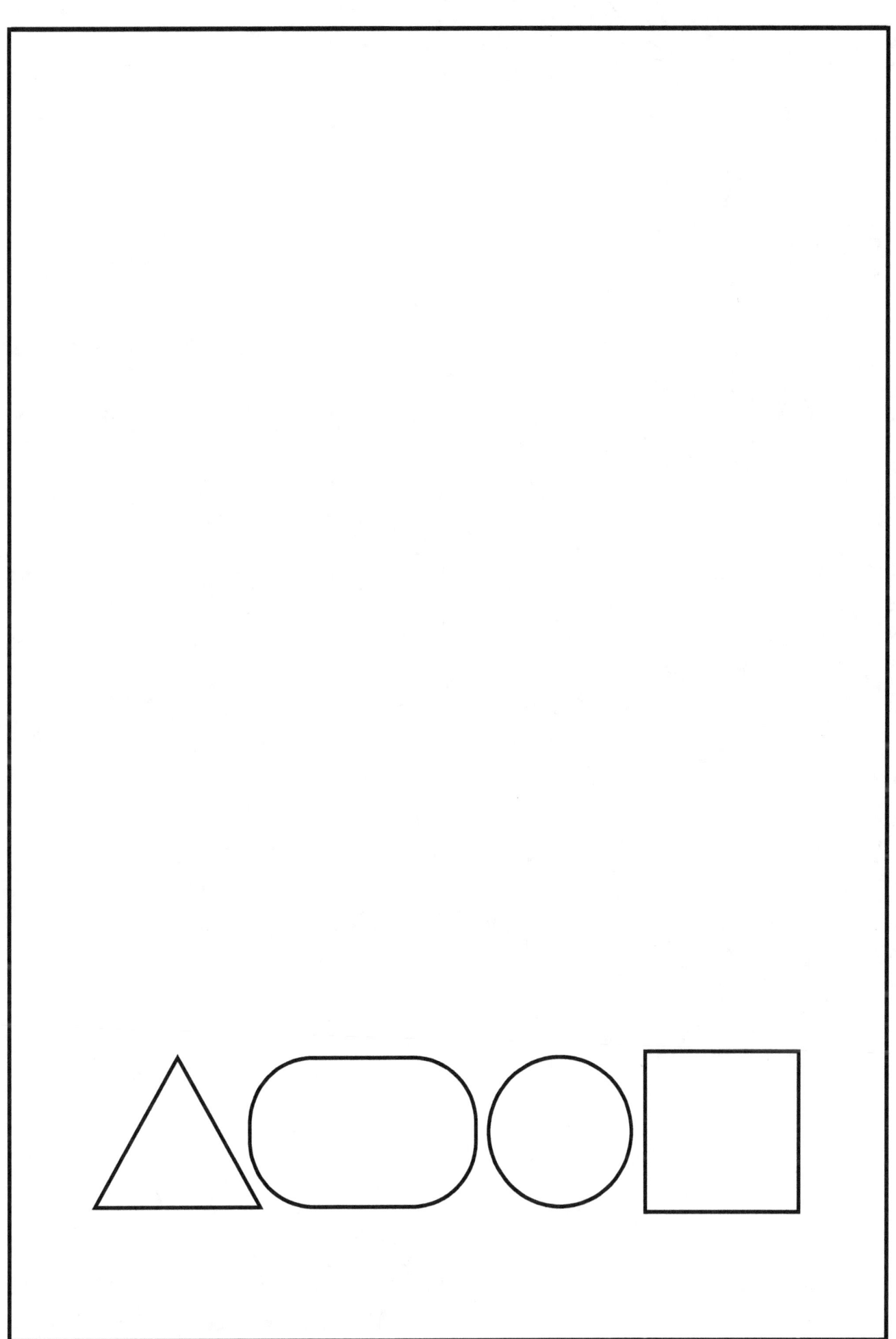

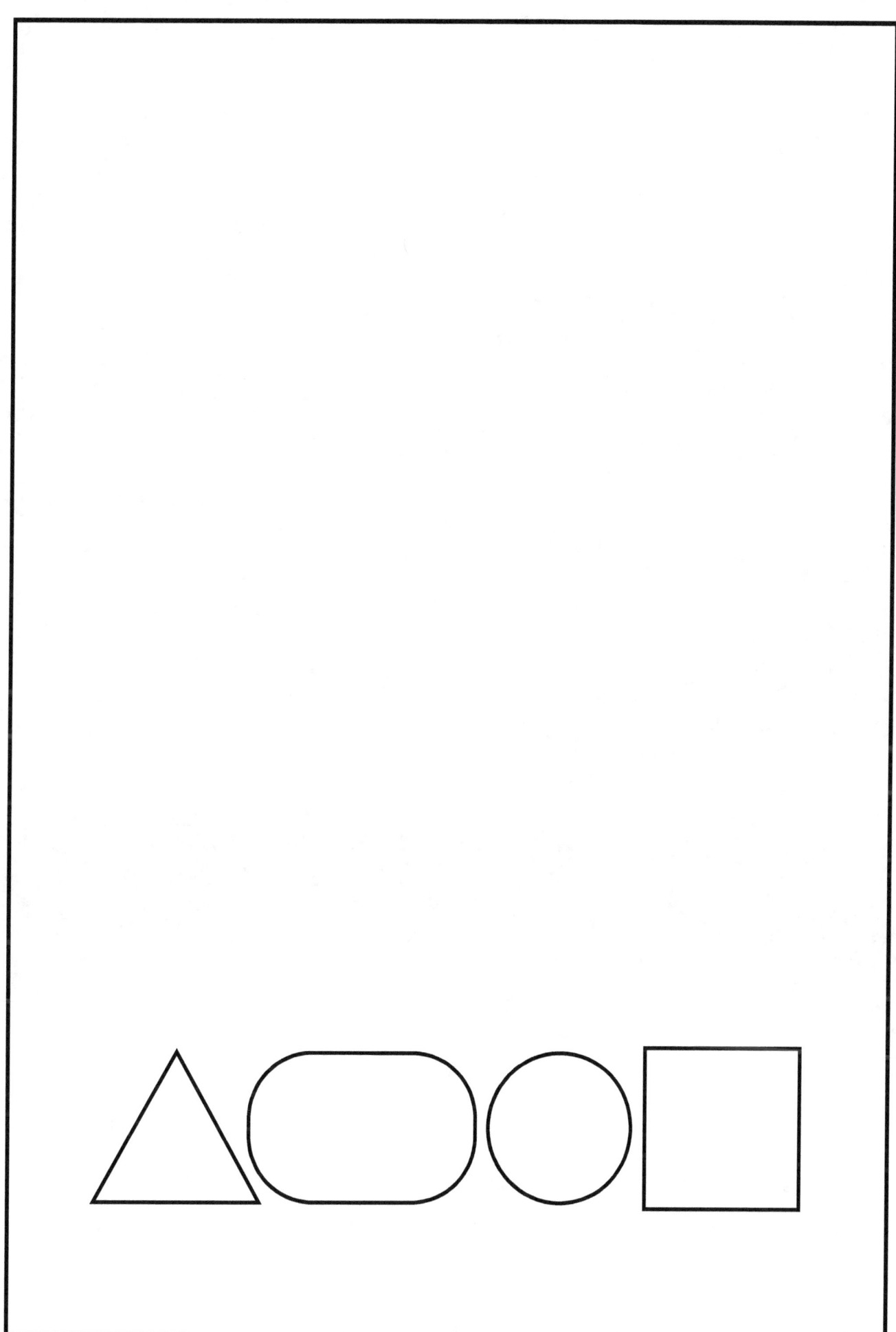

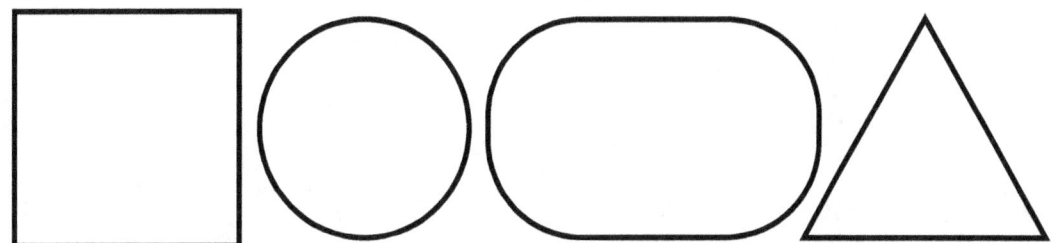

I hoped you enjoyed this book.

For more information, please visit:

www.mary-margaretmarx.com

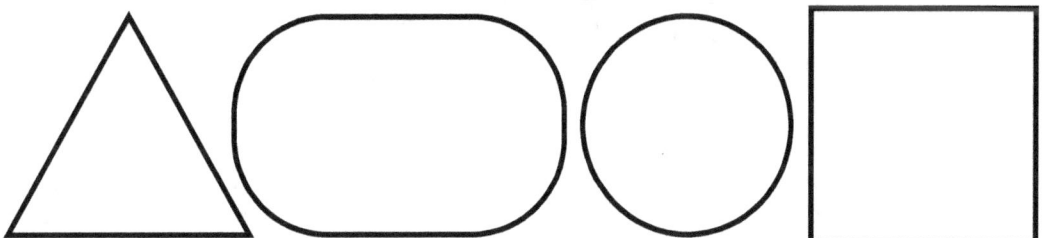